Praise for *The Growth CFO Void* and Kirk W. McLaren

Foresight is our entire financial management and accounting operation. Outsourcing is a dangerous thing unless you have a company that you trust. We are dealing with money; if something goes wrong, it can go very wrong. That affects your ability to pay taxes, pay your employees, and know if you are making a profit.

The good news is that I could not be more thrilled with Foresight. Their block-and-tackle accounting is rock solid, plus they are proactive about pointing out the next steps. That's what you want—a proactive partner.

Another thing that I love is that they are strategic CFOs. They sit down with me to figure out how to increase the value of my company, how to save, and better ways to make money. It's a great value. Give 'em a shot.

—Richard Rossi
CEO, DaVinci Education
Former President, Envision EMI

We have had the privilege and good fortune to work with Foresight CFO for several years now. Kirk and his team's insights have been incredibly valuable to help us improve and grow our business. Following their strategies, we have increased top and bottom-line growth, experiencing 80 percent revenue growth in 2021 alone. There is no question—we are stronger with the Foresight CFO on our team.

—**Gar Whaley**
President, Aligned Technology Solutions

I cannot say enough about how valuable Foresight CFO was for us. We brought them in right as we started growing and they guided us through our rapid growth and eventual exit.

I recommend Foresight to all my colleagues and friends and hope to be able to employ and/or partner with them again in my next endeavor.

—**Rob Daly**
CEO, Stelligent

I have had the privilege of working with Kirk and his leadership team for several years now. They have always been fiercely focused on supporting the needs of their clients, helping to stretch their thinking and guide them on the path to growth. Foresight is a category leader when it comes to financial management, and I encourage everyone to learn how they can help you take your business to the next level.

—**Jaime Nespor Zawmon**
President, Titan CEO
Former President, SmartCEO Magazine

I have known and worked with Kirk since 2015. From the beginning I sensed that Kirk was born to drive business growth. Foresight CFO has had enviable growth since we first talked about common experiences in business.

I have personally seen Kirk help many dozens of companies break through on their growth path. Any CEO that earnestly seeks to find breakthroughs for the next level of growth will find ample challenging ideas and follow-through working with Foresight CFO. As Kirk puts it, you will learn how to Obliterate the Obstacles to Growth with the numbers.

—Henri Schauffler
CEO Coach, CEO Focus

As a nonprofit, financial management and good forecasting are a challenge. Until we partnered with Foresight CFO, I spent a lot of sleepless nights worrying whether I had a true understanding of our financial position and what might be around the bend that I had not anticipated. Foresight CFO changed all of that. I am now confident in our current financial management and our ability to predict where we are headed into the future! No more surprises!

—Scott Jensen
Executive Director, NVSBC

The analytical, thoughtful approach provided by Foresight CFO breathed meaningful insight into our business for developing plans to increase valuation and reduce risk. The effort clarified our strategic direction.

—Robert E. Pollin
CEO, Autoscribe

I have worked with Kirk for thirty years. He epitomizes trustworthiness, strong character, an extraordinary work ethic, and is a super person to boot. I consider myself exceptionally lucky to have gotten to know Kirk and to be able to count on him as a trusted and reliable fiduciary and friend. I have recommended his firm many times and remain a longstanding customer today. His wisdom and growth practice have been of priceless value to me personally and to my operating entities. He's been vital to building and maintaining momentum and enhancing profitability.

—S. Blake Swensrud II
WorldCell

I have had the pleasure of working with Foresight CFO since late 2019. After our initial conversation with CEO Kirk W. McLaren, we decided to engage their services. Needless to say, we never looked back. Foresight's services have played an invaluable role in helping me to establish significant financial controls at the company. Under their watchful eye, particularly that of our virtual CFO José Villarino, we have maintained cost controls for the last two plus years and produced meaningful financials, including fine detail that accounts for every dollar of revenue and expense as well as tracking important trend health indicators such as EBITDA and forecast models. Foresight was extremely instrumental in helping us achieve our PPP and Main Street funding facilities. We highly recommend Foresight CFO and its group of professionals.

—Ricardo Brooks
COO, Allied Telecom Group

Many mid-career students were intimidated by the financial management course until Kirk taught it. Kirk's ability to take complicated material and teach it in a way that makes sense to technology managers and business leaders at Georgetown demonstrates his ability to connect on a personal level. His teaching style resonates with students.

—Beverly Magda

Dean, Georgetown University SCS

Kirk infuses clarity and confidence with his teaching approach for building solution-oriented financial habits for new and experienced executives. His formula is practical for the here-and-now and provides a road map for the future. His ability to translate financial planning, budgeting, and implementation strategies to leaders from a wide range of backgrounds and industries is impressive. Our organization has witnessed this firsthand with Kirk's teaching in our entrepreneurial-focused business program.

—Jaime Feeman

Dog Tag Director, Georgetown University

Being a small firm where a CEO may still wear many hats, Foresight CFO quickly became a trusted partner that took the time to understand our business and has helped transition us through the numbers for exponential growth. This gave us a clear understanding of where we are and focused us on areas that would spur not only short-term results but a game plan going forward.

—Chris Kelly

CEO and President, Kelmar Safety, Inc.

I wasn't getting what I needed from accounting. Now that I've worked with Foresight, I know my cash at the beginning of the week and get a management report at the end of the week listing what was done and what will be done next week. Not only do I get monthly financial statements on time, but they also provide me with a dashboard-style analysis. Foresight was a lifesaver.

—Technology CEO
Washington, DC

Foresight CFO's monthly value-building program changed how I work. By the second quarter, opportunities replaced fires as I invested in the scalable part of my business. I learned to use my financials and the peer benchmarks to make competitive decisions that I didn't even know about before. Just by achieving the average inventory turn, I freed up $627,000 in cash.

—Food Distributor President
Sacramento, California

Foresight CFO corrected a year of messy accounting records in three weeks then kept getting better. For the first time, the bank extended me a line of credit based on the reliability of my numbers. Then we got into the good stuff, using a strategic CFO to grow my topline and bottom-line.

—Education CEO
Austin, Texas

Our Foresight CFO provided financial benchmark insights into our strategic planning process. We compared ourselves to the industry, then used a long-term forecast to figure out where we needed to be and where we needed to start this year to maximize our valuation. Working together monthly helped us understand cost and pricing options as we improved sales and built the capacity that supports our growing business. Profit has increased 38 percent already, and the operational audit produced $1.23 million in cost savings.

—**Sports Healthcare President**
Chicago, Illinois

As two independent specialty/hybrid pharmacies in the greater New York area, we have been engaged with Foresight CFO for just about a year now. During that time, we have worked mostly with Growth CFO José Villarino, who has assisted us diligently and insightfully to get our accounting system and general financial health in order so that we would be well-positioned for our exit strategy, for which we had set an 18-month timeline.

José helped us implement a cash flow forecast which was updated with his help and guidance on a weekly basis, a long-term financial projection, and weekly consults to keep us on track and moving forward. His advice and counsel have proven to be invaluable to our positioning for a successful exit that is so far on schedule.

Overall, I would rate our experience with Foresight CFO as exemplary and have found it both cost-effective and essential to reaching our business goals.

—**Pharmacy CEO**
New York, New York

We were burning $450,000 a month and owed global telecom service providers $8 million in unpaid billings with no end in sight. I asked Kirk, who is a friend from twenty years ago who ran my financial operation at another company, to step in. Thankfully he did. We quickly restructured the business to break even then make a profit, and he negotiated with the telecom companies to discharge the debt. In doing so, we recapitalized the business and are thriving now.

—**Technology IoT CEO**

THE **GROWTH CFO** VOID

KIRK W. McLAREN

THE **GROWTH CFO** VOID

The Guide to What's Holding You Back
FROM BECOMING A 2% CEO

ForbesBooks

Published by ForbesBooks, Charleston, South Carolina.
Member of Advantage Media Group.

ForbesBooks is a registered trademark, and the ForbesBooks colophon is a trademark of Forbes Media, LLC.

Printed in the United States of America.

10 9 8 7 6 5 4 3 2 1

ISBN: 978-1-95086-390-7
LCCN: 2022903230

This custom publication is intended to provide accurate information and the opinions of the author in regard to the subject matter covered. It is sold with the understanding that the publisher, Advantage|ForbesBooks, is not engaged in rendering legal, financial, or professional services of any kind. If legal advice or other expert assistance is required, the reader is advised to seek the services of a competent professional.

Advantage Media Group is proud to be a part of the Tree Neutral® program. Tree Neutral offsets the number of trees consumed in the production and printing of this book by taking proactive steps such as planting trees in direct proportion to the number of trees used to print books. To learn more about Tree Neutral, please visit **www.treeneutral.com**.

Since 1917, Forbes has remained steadfast in its mission to serve as the defining voice of entrepreneurial capitalism. ForbesBooks, launched in 2016 through a partnership with Advantage Media Group, furthers that aim by helping business and thought leaders bring their stories, passion, and knowledge to the forefront in custom books. Opinions expressed by ForbesBooks authors are their own. To be considered for publication, please visit **www.forbesbooks.com**.

This book is dedicated to the global TrueTEAM members who step into the unknown to go beyond what any one person could know or do on their own.

Contents

Acknowledgments

I'd like to take a moment and acknowledge the people who have played a significant role in conceiving this book.

A big thanks to my father and mother, Don and Patricia McLaren. As a salesman and educator respectively, they taught me decency and a strong work ethic that started this journey.

My business partners John Redmond, José J. Villarino, Rahul Sancheti, and Sanket Shah worked closely to reimagine what CFOs can do to contribute to CEOs doing well and having peace of mind.

S. Blake Swensrud II is a telecom entrepreneur. He was my first boss post-Army and coming back from Venezuela. Blake is able to anticipate things to come with remarkable accuracy. And twenty years later, he was Foresight's first customer before we really became a company.

Richard Rossi, whose business culture encouraged entrepreneurship through fresh, creative thinking and gratitude impacted me more than he may know.

Dave Laposata is the most remarkable COO/CFO I ever worked with. His unique skills are making complicated operations easy and communicating to audiences in a manner that works for them.

Henri Schauffler was my CEO Coach from CEO Focus. I began working with Henri two months before incorporating Foresight. I knew from experience that CEOs with strong chief-level collaboration do better than those without, and Henri taught me so much. In fact, Henri introduced me to my partner John Redmond.

Jaime Zawmon, the president of Titan CEO, coached me and my management team to greater execution for years. Jaime joined us as a member of the 2% CEO Mastermind peer group to build her business.

That is where Paul Berman stepped in as our 2% CEO Mastermind coach when Jaime passed the torch. Paul is a pure no-excuse doer. The Navy SEALs could take a page out of Paul's playbook to do even better. As a result, my business is supercharging.

From working with thousands of CEOs, Russell C. Teter III, the University of Maryland SBDC executive coach, helped us learn how to build businesses better. In particular, the weekly key performance indicators are a life changer.

Alf Priestley, the Certified Family Business Advisor in Australia, and Jackie Le Fevre, the Director of Magma Effect in the United Kingdom, helped us start a journey to know and live up to our values as well as learn that teaching is one of our competitive advantages.

John Williamson in Scotland and Josh Rhodes are the communication consultants that brought obliterating obstacles to the forefront.

Our book is the specific result of Steve Scholl, who introduced me to Mark Richardson, who shared his experience publishing. Their experience and encouragement led to my introduction to Adam Witty, Harper Tucker, and Rusty Shelton at Advantage|ForbesBooks.

Good people collaborating and working side by side together— you know what they say, one thing leads to another. This is how Foresight and this book came to be.

About the Author

Kirk W. McLaren is the CEO of Foresight CFO and a graduate studies lecturer at Georgetown University School of Continuing Studies.

Kirk's love for privately owned businesses, military experience, and teaching skill led to the development of the Habits of Profitability™. His team develops selected financial talent into Growth CFOs who work side by side with CEOs across the full journey, from foundation to succession options. In doing so, CEOs gain clarity and confidence about the right bold moves along with follow-through impact while protecting the CEO from downside.

Kirk is married to the love of his life, Nayarit, and has two sons, Don Fernando and Luke Leonardo, who are both serving as Army officers by way of West Point Military Academy. The family includes two Belgian Malinois who are incredibly smart and athletic.

Kirk served in the US Army as a behavioral scientist during the first Gulf War. He is bilingual (Spanish-English).

Kirk holds an MBA with a finance and accounting concentration, an MA in international relations and economics from Johns Hopkins SAIS, a graduate certificate in international business from Georgetown University, and a BS from University of Maryland University College; is a licensed certified public accountant (CPA) and a certified treasury professional (CTP); and earned his impact financial management (IFM) certification.

BORN TO DRIVE BUSINESS GROWTH

Where do you suppose I first got the advanced training that helped prepare me to start a company that guides other CEOs of small to medium-sized private businesses to success? It wasn't Harvard Business School—not even close. That training in behavioral science happened at Fort Sam Houston in my home state of Texas. I was 21 years old when I joined the Army during the Gulf War, which began in 1991 after Iraq invaded Kuwait. I had dropped out of Texas A&M University and done my eight weeks of Army Basic Training at Fort Knox after taking the aptitude test that would determine my eligibility to learn an Army specialized skill.

The career I seemed destined for as a teenager and focused on in college was business. Today, I would say I was born to drive business growth. The Army aptitude test seemed to have a few other ideas: mortuary science. Where did that come from? Counterintelligence. That would have been cool, but they found out I can't distinguish red and green colors well enough to keep from mixing up the wires if I needed to deactivate a bomb. And so, I chose behavioral science, which landed me at the prestigious Walter Reed Army Medical Center (now the Walter Reed National Military Medical Center), located then in Washington, DC. My job description included secondary skill combat medic, but at Walter Reed I was far away from the bullets and explosions.

Today, I would say I was born to drive business growth.

It turned out that behavioral science work for the Army, with its focus on making authentic connections with people, was an excellent foundation for my business career. It is all about people.

The military is objective driven. My objective was to use my training to help the Army determine whether, when, and how it could send hospitalized soldiers back into the field. I was part of a clinical team. We all worked side by side, regardless of rank. We learned from each other, and there was an emphasis on continuous learning. The doctors, nurses, and psychologists were important members of the team, but they couldn't do their jobs when in the field without the synergy of others handling logistics, transporting personnel, and keeping the troops in the field fed and supplied. Most important, we kept each other fully informed, so nobody could develop a blind spot.

I enjoyed getting out into the wards, doing the day-to-day evaluations and therapeutic treatment, and contacting the service members' families, because I like being with all different kinds of people. I was doing the initial psychosocial assessments of the hospitalized soldiers, and I found many of them to be gung ho about getting back to the front lines, even if they were not in fighting shape. Some had abused alcohol or drugs, others were injured, and I remember one good soldier, Jason, who sadly had a sudden and extreme onset of schizophrenia. Jason was one of the warrior types, a decent Midwestern kid who really wanted to return to active duty but never would be able to. He was struggling to understand why he was at a hospital when he was so motivated to be with his unit.

This description of a rattled warrior may seem out of place in a book about using financial management CFO skills to Obliterate Obstacles to Growth. It's not. Lessons from my military service echo throughout this book: just as in my years in the business world, I encountered a lot of competitive people with a drive to win. But they were not always ready for the battlefield. To be properly equipped, they needed clear objectives, well-placed confidence, and the synergies of teamwork. On the TrueTEAM that I will be describing in this book, everyone takes ownership of their individual responsibilities, and the Growth CFO takes extreme ownership.[1] We work together to create practical options based on what motivates and moves the CEOs we are helping.

This is a business book for and about people, not products or services. I always have been interested in how people learn, develop, and behave. After my military experience showed me the value of continuous learning, with people from different backgrounds and with different expertise and responsibilities learning side by side, I went back to school. I got my college degree in Maryland while completing my active duty on nights and weekends, and after leaving the military I earned two master's degrees—one in international relations and economics and the other an MBA with a finance and accounting area of expertise. In between I went to Venezuela for about a year to learn Spanish and teach English, and that's where I met my wife, Nayarit. I then worked in business, starting in financial management, and in addition I later became a graduate school adjunct professor of

---

1   *Extreme Ownership*, a best-selling 2019 book by former Navy SEALs Jocko Willink and Leif Babin, popularized this term for a no-excuses leadership mindset.

financial management at Georgetown University School of Continuing Studies in Washington, DC.

My first foray into business leadership was motivated by a desire to study martial arts when I was a high school sophomore. I started a lawn maintenance business with two buddies to pay for lessons. We were in the part of the Houston-area suburban sprawl, where enough houses were packed into each block that a three-person team could earn $20 in as little as 10 minutes mowing a lawn. We had no problem getting customers without advertising because we showed up on time and did a great job. We enjoyed the challenge of growing the business, and within three years we ended up with 1,500 customers and 75 employees. We were grossing about $1.2 million per year. Acquiring and deploying trucks and keeping track of all the equipment, employees, and customers were intellectually stimulating, like doing a puzzle. We figured out a cost-saving way of running three crews off one truck. In hindsight, we tripled the return on asset. The parents of one of my partners eventually took over the business because it was more profitable than what they had been doing in their careers.

Years later, when I started teaching graduate courses at Georgetown, I had to break down the Habits of Profitability I had learned into lessons for nonfinancial managers. I realized I had a system that I wanted to share with business leaders, which led me to incorporate Foresight CFO. In the first half of this book, I will introduce you to the particular types of executives who are more likely or less likely to benefit from our system. You will learn why Foresight CFO recruits and trains what we call Growth CFOs to work side by side with growth-oriented CEOs who need clarity about next steps and strong follow-through. Then, in the second half of the book, I will explain the FIVE Habits of Profitability and what the exceptional CEOs taking advantage of this proven system gain along the way.

Some CEOs are not a good fit for our approach, which requires an open, learning mindset and a willingness to challenge the status quo. They may be too reluctant to shine a light on blind spots or to embrace our use of numbers to chart a path forward. Their relationship with a Growth CFO requires people being both authentic and vulnerable to develop mutual trust. Back when the Army decided I should be in behavioral science, I was not surprised, because I knew I had an ability to understand and connect with different personality types and deeply care about people doing well on multiple levels. When I am getting to know the CEOs that my company is helping, I enjoy finding out what motivates them. They are not all conquer-the-world warriors. Some are motivated to do well by doing good, which is also characteristic of the Foresight CFO company culture. They take good care of their own people and their customers or clients.

The CEOs we work well with tend to value and seek the same leadership qualities that we admire: clarity, confidence, vivid vision, a drive to have impact, and being bold in thoughtful ways—to deliver a *wow* factor and a willingness to challenge the status quo. They hope to grow their business to be the best, not the biggest. Some are already thinking about a succession plan and, even before they pass the torch, having more time for family or other interests. Working from home during the COVID-19 pandemic seemed to be a tipping point for some CEOs whose long hours had taken a personal toll. The Habits of Profitability are aimed not only at growth but also getting time back for the people and things that matter personally.

When I realized during my teaching how challenged many non-financial executives are when it comes to using numbers, I saw a solution and a business opportunity to work with CEOs globally. I founded a company with a unique structure and process that I will explain in the final chapters of this book. First, however, let's focus on what motivates and what troubles the CEOs of many small to medium-sized private businesses.

WE VALUE:

Being a TrueTEAM Member: Knowing that the sum is greater than the parts, we take extreme ownership to learn best practices and deliver through teams. We support and encourage one another to give our best, and we always have each other's back.

Judgment-driven "wow": Applying our wisdom and experience, we approach every task with thought and skill, enabling us to achieve goals and impacts that delight clients who become raving fans.

Speaking up: Cultivating mutual trust and confidence, we seek and share feedback candidly, we participate actively, and proactively speak up when we get stuck. This gives us "speed of trust" advantages.

Continuous mastery: Learning is a lifelong pursuit; we deliberately work individually and collectively to develop our talents, capabilities, and contributions.

Do well by doing good: Using the right tools, the right way, we rally around providing a positive impact for business, people, and community in such a way that our team members thrive.

CHAPTER 1

UNDERSTANDING THE CEO'S MOTIVATION

F rom the lowliest beggar in the streets to the celebrated entre-preneur raising capital in the C-suites, anyone asking someone else for money should have a good story to tell. I was fortunate that the first company where I served as a vice president for finance, starting in 2005, had a great story to tell about its mission and purpose. Envision EMI was a fast-growing creator of professional and leadership programs for high-achieving young people. Providing enrichment and leadership programs for high school students gifted in math, music, or other fields could be the purview of a nonprofit, but Richard Rossi and Barbara Harris cofounded Envision as a privately held for-profit company that managed nonprofit education programs. Harris, who passed away in 2012, about a year before the company was sold, started as a public schoolteacher in New York and Connecti-cut. Rossi had been a US Senate staffer. Their company's founding was inspired by the benefits Harris saw her students get from a field trip to the nation's capital that she arranged with the help of a congressional staffer during President Ronald Reagan's second inauguration.

The company did well by doing good, because it was exceptionally well managed by the leadership management team that Rossi cultivated as CEO. I saw firsthand that Envision put on great programs; my children attended them, and long afterward they would spontaneously bring up lessons learned. That type of enrichment programming could be done on a small scale. But thinking small would not have fit Rossi's growth-oriented leadership style. I was with Envision less than six years, and during that time revenue quadrupled to nine figures. That doesn't just happen by luck.

Rossi was motivated to build the world's largest experiential learning program. Its successful growth was rooted in parents being able to clearly see its value. If your high school son or daughter was thinking about going into medicine, for example, a program in which they could interact with med students and doctors, watch live surgery, and otherwise be immersed in the field would help the family decide whether they were on the right path before investing in their higher education. I think Envision programs deserve some credit for both my sons being accepted and succeeding at the US Military Academy at West Point. (My Army mentor, Sgt. Joseph C. Sharpe Jr., who became the godfather to my children, also was instrumental, along with Nayarit. I cannot overstate the role Joseph Sharpe's friendship has played in our lives.)

> *I was with Envision less than six years, and during that time revenue quadrupled to nine figures. That doesn't just happen by luck.*

The company's profitability benefited from strategic financial planning. The business leaders guided managers in a process of budgeting and reporting that became like a scoreboard showing how the financial numbers reflected whether they were helping fulfill the CEO's objectives. The chief operating officer and CFO, Dave Laposata, was both a tough boss and mentor who showed me how to supercharge business growth and how to communicate technical details and broader context to different audiences. Dave influenced my thinking about the importance of making sure the managers understood where their numbers fit into the big picture. My part of the work as VP Finance included operational analysis that identified ways to achieve more than $1 million in annual savings, which translated into $1 million in profit and at least $6 million in the value of the business. Along the way I absorbed many lessons applicable to any growth-oriented private company.

This book will explain what these companies must do to increase revenue and profitability and gain clarity and confidence to make well-informed decisions about how to spend and invest their resources. We will address business owners' needs for peace of mind and time to focus on the activities most valuable to them personally as well as to their companies. You will learn about Obliterating Obstacles to Growth, what we at Foresight CFO call the FIVE Habits of Profitability, and how to Get Paid Twice. But first, I have found that examining the business leader's motivation is the best starting point. Are you, like Rossi, motivated to build the biggest and best company of your type? Or are you more like some other CEOs that I will introduce you to in this chapter?

CPA FIRM PARTNERS

Like any private company owner who is dealing with pressures from competition and technology, a certified public accountant (CPA) firm should be planning long term to overcome obstacles to its business growth. Just because the partners have the aptitude with numbers to do audit and tax work does not mean they are filling the CFO role for themselves. They may have a lot to learn about the reality and potential of their revenue sources. Chapter 4 addresses that opportunity.

Three Types of CEOs

John Warrillow, author of *Built to Sell: Creating a Business That Can Thrive Without You*, suggested there are three types of business owners, which he dubbed the Freedom Fighters, the Mountain Climbers, and Craftspeople.[2] He concluded from his research that about 75 percent of business owners are Craftspeople, absorbed by the work they do and motivated toward perfecting it. Most of the rest are Freedom Fighters, motivated by independence and driven to live life on their own terms. Then there are the elite Mountain Climbers whose strong motivations make them most likely to be able to build a business that stands out as the first, the largest, or the best.

I read Warrillow's book several years ago during a period when I was working as CFO for a telecom company but thinking about building a business of my own that could change how small businesses perform. The book resonated with me and gave me clarity about my own experience. I had seen CEOs trapped into working endless long days because their business was too dependent on them. I wanted to give them and myself a route to a better outcome, providing time for

---

2   John Warrillow, *Built to Sell: Creating a Business That Can Thrive Without You* (New York: Portfolio/Penguin, 2011).

the people and things we care about in life. I later completed Warrillow's certification program, and it has helped me recognize the value drivers in the businesses I work with and how these relate to the motivations of their CEOs beyond the numbers. Typical CFOs don't think much about this interrelationship, but it is important to my company's work. Using what we call a TrueTEAM approach and providing Growth CFOs, we help CEOs operate their business well and deal with succession issues, which we will describe in detail in chapter 7.

The 2% CEO

When we started working with private business owners, we needed an aspirational description of the exceptional ones who have made it but remain willing to pay for help they need developing and managing their growth plan. We came up with "The 2% CEO" during our ongoing research into our clients' thinking and the challenges they face in reaching their objectives.

Only 6 percent of business owners build a business that earns $1 million or more annually.[3] Only 48.9 percent of businesses make it past the fifth year.[4] A business that is earning seven to eight figures and is around after five years is in the top percentile. Barely 2 percent of new businesses really succeed to the extent that they stay in business for more than five years, their revenue tops $1 million, and they are not dependent on the CEO as an owner who is also wearing all the hats.

In some cases, the 2% CEOs are looking to be the biggest in their industry, but in most cases, they are looking to be the best.

---

3   Verne Harnish, *Scaling Up: How a Few Companies Make It ... and Why the Rest Don't* (Ashburn, VA: October 21, 2014).

4   US Small Business Association, "Frequently Asked Questions," accessed January 2022, https://cdn.advocacy.sba.gov/wp-content/uploads/2021/12/06095731/Small-Business-FAQ-Revised-December-2021.pdf.

They tend to share certain characteristics, including being straight talkers and needing to be heard. They self-identify as being smart and self-aware. They have an open, learning mindset, yet they struggle relating to numbers. As a result, they don't always realize how well they are doing.

In working with business owners to Obliterate Obstacles to Growth, we begin with an in-depth conversation in which we try to understand the CEO's objectives and motivations. I find they usually don't fall completely into one of Warrillow's three archetypes. However, company owners who are most purely Craftspeople, whose motivation is very focused on their product or service, have difficulty dedicating themselves to growing a business once they are pulling in sufficient income to support themselves and their family. Believing that no one can do it as well as them, they are reluctant to split up leadership roles within their companies. Business growth takes a lot of work, and they might be more fulfilled spending time collaborating with peers to make their product even better.

In some cases, the 2% CEOs are looking to be the biggest in their industry, but in most cases, they are looking to be the best.

I recall a CEO of a physical therapy company who developed innovative activities for people on the autism spectrum. That business owner had a wonderful motivation to help clients, but I was hard pressed to keep that CEO's attention during a conversation about his objective of expanding into new territories, rolling out new products, or developing a lead generation system. His true motive was building a better mousetrap and nothing more, which is fine. The Mountain Climbers are at the opposite end of the spectrum, highly motivated to work on business growth—conquering the mountain, figuratively speaking. Richard Rossi is a good example of that type of business founder. He would be as excited looking at a chart of revenue numbers as he would discussing his mission of helping young people explore careers and learn about leadership.

The Freedom Fighters want to build a respectable business that is not dependent on them, whether it is for the sake of themselves, their families, their customers, or all three. They are motivated not to be the biggest or best company so much as live life on their own terms. They want to grow their revenue and plan early for the desired outcomes we will discuss in chapters 6 and 7: growing profitability and getting paid twice. Hard work making a company profitable pays off in real time, and again in the future when effective succession planning results in a lucrative acquisition or other exit strategy. They want to move on and enjoy the financial freedom to do whatever they want to do. But not all Freedom Fighters are forward thinking enough and willing to put in the work involved in getting there. And not all Mountain Climbers are successful at building their empire.

It Gets Personal

Viewing business owners' motivations through these broad classifications is helpful, but when we meet personally with CEOs, we take a much deeper dive into their objectives. Many of them fear communicating too clearly about their objectives because doing so makes them accountable. They may have developed a habit of setting low objectives to manage expectations. Other CEOs will boldly announce aspirational objectives for their company but be reluctant to share details of their personal motivations. How much household income do they need? Are they worried about putting their children through college because they have invested so much of their savings in their business? Why do they spend so much time working, and how is it affecting their lives?

Conversely, many CEOs enjoy talking about their personal motivations once we broach the subject. They tell us about a deep commitment to do something for their family, community, employees, or others. They revel in turning clients into raving fans. Or they explain how what they are doing makes them feel they have fulfilled a destiny and led a worthwhile life.

The CEO's personal objectives invariably intersect with business objectives. Wanting more free time requires building a management team. Deciding what the CEO should be doing on a day-to-day basis requires thinking about the desired scope of the business. How does the current client response feel? What locations and geographic service areas, top-line revenue, and profitability compared with industry peers would be ideal? Aligning actions with objectives requires a vivid vision of what the CEO wants and why that outcome is important to them. Without that alignment, the CEO is less likely to see options, explore potential bold moves, and follow through with implementation.

Build It to Sell?

The Freedom Fighter type is neither coasting toward retirement nor trying to conquer the world but simply has other interests outside of the business. In the technology industry, we see midcareer CEOs who build a business intending to sell it in a few years or several years and then start another one. One CEO I know typifies the technology engineer mindset that you build something to sell it. What you build doesn't have to be the biggest, the best, or perfect, as long as it is valuable to someone, so they are willing to buy it at a good price. That type of CEO tends to focus on the day-to-day running of the business, to maintain high standards, but also keeps a constant eye out for the next step or advancement. They are like software developers who want to deliver an update regularly for business reasons, in contrast with the Craftspeople who are motivated by a desire to perfect the product. They may have in the back of their minds a short list of potential strategic buyers for their business. That prospect is a motivation for creating a business that is not dependent on them.

By their nature these serial entrepreneurs may enjoy the freedom of knowing they can take time off. The technology engineer CEO I mentioned, Rob Daly, likes to get away when the weather's good for a bicycle ride. In fact, he got me into mountain biking, and we ride together almost weekly in and around Washington, DC, and along the Potomac River. The successful business owners I have met are all hard working. As I get to know them, I realize some, maybe one in four, see that hard work as a means to an end in which they have the time and resources to live out their personal dreams.

An Unprofitable Management Style

One all-work-and-no-play CEO I encountered, who probably falls into the category of failed Mountain Climber, always was putting out fires. He was very good at developing his business as a government contractor. But he neglected the foundational work involved in making the business profitable. I'll fully explain in chapter 6 what a CEO must do to develop the FIVE Habits of Profitability. In this case, the CEO didn't have managers keeping track of revenue, profit and loss, and cash flow. He didn't have financial reports that he could literally take to the bank.

Maybe he had skeletons in the closet such as tax liabilities that he wanted to keep hidden, but he also didn't like to delegate authority.

He liked having the business dependent upon his coming in each morning and responding to the fire alarm. Something was always on fire because of the company's chaotic, ad hoc management. It was a disorganized business, where meetings started late or ran long, where getting anything decided required top-level involvement. This company had close to $100 million in revenue at one point, but it could not fulfill its growth potential without officers or department heads taking ownership of their areas. The company was well positioned to be profitable because it could take advantage of set-aside programs to win government contracts, but instead its revenue slid back 90 percent. That failure is an extreme case of lax financial management. However, there are plenty of situations in which a company doesn't have to do anything particularly well to win contracts or become established in a niche market without putting proper financial management in place.

Spending Money to Make Money

To help you understand why I have begun this book discussing motivation, let me explain what happened when our TrueTEAM began working with one particular information technology company. The CEO expressed a desire to grow the business from about $2 million in annual revenue to as big as $20 million. That objective was realistic, because its services were in demand to respond to cybersecurity threats, but there was an obstacle to overcome. The entry-level bookkeeping system the company was using required too much manual effort to support that kind of growth. The company needed clarity about where it stood each month and how it was progressing toward its long-term objectives.

We knew we could save this company a lot of money facilitating the necessary move to a true enterprise software system that could handle everything from e-commerce, staffing, and inventory to profit-and-loss reporting allocated by profit center. The CEO made a big, high-cost decision to start such an upgrade, which involves spending months uprooting and replacing the accounting system that ties together the components of a business. The company would be undergoing surgery on its central nervous system. Its people's roles and day-to-day responsibilities would change. They would have to develop and learn new processes. But the effort made sense because it suited their CEO's motivation toward large-scale growth.

Five Obstacles to Growth

Obstacles to business growth come in all kinds of shapes and sizes. What they have in common is that they stand in the way of some basic business objectives. Ask CEOs about the biggest obstacles they want to overcome, and the answer almost always falls into one or more of these five categories we'll discuss in the pages ahead:

1. Winning new customers

2. Proactively gaining access to capital

3. Having the right people and capacity to deliver

4. Keeping and growing existing customers

5. Low financial performance

You have learned so far about different CEOs of small or medium-sized private companies and their varying approaches to seeking growth. We also discussed three different types of business leaders and how the largest group, the Craftspeople, are least inclined toward doing the work to obliterate obstacles by adopting the habits needed for profitable growth. Every CEO doesn't fit neatly into one of the three archetypes because any individual's motivation stems from personal needs and circumstances. Starting off by understanding motivation and then asking about personal and business objectives is how we at Foresight CFO customize a plan to overcome Obstacles to Growth. We meet business owners who are clearly motivated to be 2% CEOs because they are the Mountain Climber types or because they are Freedom Fighters trying to build something they can sell. We also meet business owners who feel trapped because they have created a company too dependent on their working long hours.

I'll explain in the next few chapters how common it is for a growth-oriented business owner to realize one day, or during a sleepless night, that they are lacking clarity and confidence in the company's financial position. Many CEOs of small businesses can be happy and successful focusing on their product or service and not worry too much about revenue growth and profitability. But for the CEOs who are focused on revenue, for the growth or freedom it promises, they need guidance in how to take on obstacles and use financial management to ensure they achieve their goals. The next chapter drills down into some factors that create Obstacles to Growth by getting in the way of a CEO's clarity and confidence.

CHAPTER 2

ARE YOU STUCK?

My first real management job was at a telecommunications company that had adopted digital technology at a time when most of the US mobile telephone infrastructure relied on analog channels. Overseas carriers, especially in Europe, were ahead in going digital. I was the revenue assurance manager at a US company, meaning I was doing analytics with better data than what was available to my company's domestic competitors. For someone like me, that edge was exciting. Working closely with our technology staff to generate reports, I could catch costly fraud in real time. I could use trend numbers in international point-to-point calling to predict how targeted price increases would disproportionately improve revenue. I could show my boss exactly how much my work was increasing profitability and the value of the business.

Some 20 years later, that telecom boss called me for some help. I had been out of the telecom industry for a long time, but he and I had stayed in touch, getting together for an occasional lunch. We both had kids who were about the same age, so we could relate to each other's lives. He trusted that he could confide in me more than his industry colleagues because I never had a separate agenda. And he had what seemed to be a revenue problem. He had sold the original telecom at a good price point and started an Internet of Things business that relied on the same core network. It was several years past the start-up phase and still burning through cash paying its employees and vendors because its product was not yet operational. The staff was demoralized. Fortunately for my old boss, I was looking for a new challenge after recently resigning from a nonprofit in disappointment over its troublesome practices.

I came in as the chief operating officer since there already was a CFO—but he was not there for long. I realized the CFO was just paying invoices, whether or not the vendors had built out the required network or technology operating platform. Hundreds of thousands of dollars were going toward expensive, proprietary equipment that didn't work as well as what we could have gotten off the shelf. As I will explain in more detail in chapter 4, traditional CFOs often operate in a void. They may perform their accounting oversight duties accurately and thoroughly, but they definitely do not see obliterating obstacles to profitability or strategic planning as part of their job description. Soon, I became the CEO's Growth CFO, a role that became a key part of the business model for the company I launched in 2014. Our efforts to end the cash burn were ultimately successful. We cut our losses by shutting down the outmoded part of the business and concentrating our resources on being a network capacity provider. When I left and incorporated my company in 2016, the twice-former boss became a client of ours.

His company was far from alone in navigating the business equivalent of river rapids, where speeding ahead also risks running aground. We have since worked with hundreds of CEOs across numerous industries in the English-speaking world who felt stuck for various reasons we will cover in this chapter. What these CEOs of small to medium-sized private businesses have in common is a feeling that they have no clarity into what is happening with their revenue and expenses or the financial course of their journey, and no confidence on how to fix it. A lot of CEOs find analytics tedious, confusing, or intimidating, and that's okay because it's not their job. But they do need to recognize warning signs that come in various shapes and sizes. With the right help, CEOs should have a big picture view into the Five Obstacles to Growth. All businesses need and care about these five things, but when something goes sideways and the CEOs can't figure out why, they feel stuck.

Top-Line Growth

Winning new clients or customers is a great cause for celebration. But how do you recognize when your company is not winning enough business to maintain adequate top-line growth—gross sales or revenue? Businesses will always lose some customers and gain some new ones, and it is a challenge to predict whether this churn will cause revenue to grow, stay flat, or decline. Perhaps sales have accelerated, but you are struggling to make sense of the financials. You are profitable—but just barely. You are not clear about the market. Should you try to sell the same product to new customers or new products to existing customers? You don't know whom to turn to for help or don't know whom you can trust. Forecasting growth potential,

A lot of CEOs find analytics tedious, confusing, or intimidating, and that's okay because it's not their job.

tracking recurring revenue, and engineering profit through pricing strategy are among the solutions we will discuss in this book.

Some common approaches that seem reliable can instead be a major source of frustration. A business may invest in promised solutions for lead generation that fail to pay off. Or it may spend a lot of money hiring and training sales employees who don't produce results. Repeated failures like these indicate a lack of capability to overcome obstacles. Without outside help to break through status quo thinking, some CEOs cannot see a path to top-line growth. The typical approach in their industry may have commoditized their products or services. Pricing below cost or close to it to win business has them feeling stuck.

Customer Retention

Do you really know how you are doing when it comes to keeping existing clients and customers? Now consider the 80/20 principle, which holds that roughly 20 percent of customers or 20 percent of marketing efforts generate 80 percent of revenue.[5] Have you identified that best 20 percent and how to grow their business or attract more of that type of best client or customer? It's not a simple head count. Tracking orders and the growth or loss of existing business over time can be complicated. Not all revenue is equally worth chasing as some is so low-profit that it can result in a business losing money once it accounts for all of the costs associated with making, selling, and delivering its goods and services. Perhaps you are in a dynamic or seasonal industry, your profit margins are fluctuating, or your clients

---

5   Many applications of the 80/20 principle have been cited over the past 125 years, but a good source for further explanation of this context is Perry Marshall, *80/20 Sales and Marketing* (Entrepreneur Press, 2013).

are merging or transforming their businesses. The economy may be in a boom or bust period or headed that way. You are not sure whether to focus on keeping and growing business among the clients you have or looking elsewhere for growth.

Keeping and growing your best customers is like reaching for low-hanging fruit, but chasing new customers often gets priority. Being too dependent on a few customers carries risks, and pursuing new ones can be exciting work. No wonder business leaders feel torn. The habits we will discuss for tracking profit and loss and analyzing customer value provide clarity.

Building Capacity

What if you can win big contracts, but then you can't do the work? Is your management team capable of handling growth? What if demand for your products or services is rising, but you can't deliver in a timely way? What if a key vendor becomes unavailable? Perhaps you can't get bonded, you can't get a line of credit, or you can't acquire the resources or hire the right people. The battle for skilled talent is intensifying in many industries. Suddenly, you are facing capacity issues that cause you to move too slowly. If you have any of these issues, and especially if sales, contracts, or service orders also are accelerating, you need a plan to get ahead of the problem.

Too many businesses fail to make wise decisions on managing capacity. The data and analysis that could help the CEO forecast demand are either nonexistent, erroneous, delayed, or lost in the daily whirlwind. There is a lot to figure out: What compensation plans work? What staffing, equipment, software, locations, and vehicles can the company afford? A CEO feels stuck when the rise and fall of demand seems random and the same mistakes in meeting demand keep recurring. In one bad scenario, the business becomes overdependent on long hours worked by the CEO or key employees, leaving them wanting out of this trap.

Access to Capital

If you don't have access to the working capital you need, you'll end up using tomorrow's money today or get mired in some of the problems we just covered: facing capacity issues, unable to retain customers, or stalled in your revenue growth. Do you know how a bank will evaluate your company's financial picture? Have you developed a good story about why your business is loan worthy? Can you obtain a line of credit to bridge the gap between payments you must make for staffing and vendors and the time you get paid by customers? Is your reserve funding adequate? Can you afford to chase opportunities such as a new territory or product? We will discuss how CEOs stuck on these questions can get answers.

Financial Performance

CEOs tend to focus on their top line, or gross revenue, and not pay sufficient attention to their bottom line, the net profit or loss. It's human nature to be more excited by new business than keeping existing customers or clients, but that's not seeing the whole picture, which also includes cash liquidity and valuation. Are you more profitable, do you have more cash in the bank, and is your company more valuable than your average competitor in the marketplace? Can you use these measures of financial performance to show you are in your sector's top percentile? Clarity about financial performance is always important strategically but especially so when a CEO is seeking a bank loan, doing succession planning, or considering a merger or acquisition from the buyer side. We'll discuss how to achieve a positive cash flow and maximize your valuation.

A CEO may feel stuck if profit margins seem too low. Some CEOs pay themselves last, which means any setbacks hit them personally. We believe in figuring in the CEO's household income requirements when setting a company's financial objectives and evaluating its performance. That evaluation requires clarity about the company's bottom line and how it compares with the industry's percentage, knowing the profitability of certain product lines, and not having to guess the value of the business. Then there is the question of why performance is lagging. Is the accounting operation sending bills late or with errors? Is money not being collected from clients? Is the business losing money by making delinquent payments, bank overdrafts, payroll errors, incorrect tax estimates, or other compliance mistakes?

No Follow-Through

Near the end of 2021, I consulted with colleagues about what issues business leaders were struggling with to help figure out what our company should focus on to help CEOs in the upcoming year. A common thread seemed to be that CEOs felt overloaded with options to address the obstacles they were facing. As a result, they didn't feel confident about making the right choices and didn't take a chance by acting on plans that had looked good to them earlier.

Paul Berman, CEO of id8 Strategies, and I were discussing why some business owners struggling to fill the top of the funnel with qualified prospects had not followed through with plans to step up marketing in 2021. They had too many options, Berman concluded, and it is human nature to put things off when uncertain. About 10 thousand miles away in Australia, another trusted advisor had similar thoughts.

In the pages ahead, we will show how to overcome the tendency to stall.

Line-of-Sight Issues

A couple of years ago, we met a CEO who had recently realized he was not confident he had an accurate picture of his company's financial performance. It turned out he was right to be concerned. His company was burning cash even though the financial reports indicated everything was okay. The sales executive and the financial executive were creating reports that basically told the CEO what he wanted to hear. The reports were not accurate, but they made everybody feel good (at least in that moment). The telecom company was privately held, so they were not obligated by law or securities regulations to have accurate financial performance reports as long as they filed their taxes correctly. Like many CEOs, however, this one was thinking a lot about how to win new customers to grow top-line revenue. He brought in a new accounting director and a chief operating officer to whip things into shape and help figure out a way forward. The COO hired Foresight CFO to create a multiyear plan with immediate reporting and drive quantitative analysis in support of decision-making.

It didn't take long for one of our experienced Growth CFOs, José J. Villarino, to see the company was good at delivering its products and services but weak on the sales side and operating in a financial management twilight zone. Operating as a peer guide and creating various turnaround mode options, José led the business on a journey of discovery and change. Needless to say, the sales executives who had been keeping the CEO in the dark had to go. That aspect was an extreme situation, but it is not unusual for CEOs to have line-of-sight issues, especially in a fast-growing business.

Many of our clients are women and men who created a product or service that found an eager audience, and they were able to grow as a leader along with their business. You may be in such a situation and suddenly feel like you are on shaky ground. Your organization has become much more complex with so many more moving parts that it is hard to keep it all in your head. When you had a smaller company, you were able to make decisions based on your gut because you could more or less see everything. Now you are attempting to see the big picture without a direct line of sight to all of the parts. Even if you are not getting inaccurate reports like our client was, your staff may not have the skills to ask the right questions and relay the right information. Most people don't speak up. Your view may still be distorted.

> *Your organization has become much more complex with so many more moving parts that it is hard to keep it all in your head.*

PEER-TO-PEER COLLABORATION

Most CEOs don't have anyone to talk with about these issues. As a company grows, members of the management team become specialized and lack an overview of the business and its place in the marketplace and with its stakeholders. A huge reason why some CEOs stay stuck is that they don't collaborate with peers to gain insights, diminish blind spots, and hold themselves accountable.

27

Growth CFOs operate as peers and guide CEOs across the
journey like a coach.

Running your start-up was like flying a single-engine Piper Cub.
You could look out the windshield to fly by using landmarks on the
ground. Now, your business has expanded, and you are flying a jetliner
with a flight crew, hundreds of passengers, and overwhelming quanti-
ties of regulations to keep up with. You can no longer fly by looking
out the window. You need advanced and highly sophisticated elec-
tronic systems and skilled team members to navigate.

When your company grows over time and gets to a certain size,
you can't keep track of it all. Now you need a management team that's
specializing in different parts of the business. It gets harder to make
decisions, because as CEO you just don't have the firsthand information that you used to have, and that can leave you feeling stuck. You
may wonder if the business is worth what you are investing in it
financially and with your personal time and freedom. Once a CEO
begins doubting their ability to make smart decisions, peace of mind
seems elusive. The joy of business ownership falls away. This book is
about ways CEOs can get unstuck—or grow with greater clarity and
confidence and feel their business is able to be the best that it can be.
Before we introduce the FIVE Habits of Profitability in the second
half of the book, we are going to discuss several human factors that
create obstacles to breaking out of an unproductive status quo.

Not Using Foresight

Disruptive trends on the horizon present another dimension of uncer-
tainty for CEOs. Even if robots are not replacing workers at their

companies yet, they must pay attention to a slew of disruptors, from artificial intelligence to cryptocurrency to the Internet of Things. My company saw the value of being ahead of the curve during COVID-19 when we watched clients struggle to do something that had been part of our business model from the start: working virtually. Technology platforms we had embraced to get the best talent and the right clients without being limited by geographical boundaries suddenly became common parts of many people's lives. Authors such as Peter H. Diamandis and Steven Kotler (*The Future Is Faster Than You Think*, Simon & Schuster, 2020) make the case that technology is accelerating exponentially, and our world will change far more and faster than we can imagine. Business leaders who don't want to feel stuck should have the foresight to plan for the inevitable displacement.

CHAPTER 3

WHAT IS KEEPING YOU THERE?

T he CEO of a frozen food shipping company was struggling to adjust its delivery capacity to match its sales potential when she came to Foresight CFO for help. My business partner, John Redmond, had seen this problem before. John has had a remarkably diverse career that exposed him to companies small and large and developed his skills in chief-level communication, technology, training, and project management. More than a decade earlier he had worked as a district sales manager for Hostess Brands, the century-old corporation that introduced iconic snack cakes including Twinkies. John knew that shipping food is a high-volume, low-margin business in which profitability relies on not missing a beat. And our new client was missing more than a beat. It was on the verge of a meltdown.

Icy Snacks (for business confidentiality reasons, that's not the company's real name) had strong sales, but its operating capacity couldn't keep up. Its support services, particularly accounting, were nonexistent. Financial record keeping was pretty much at that stage where someone starting a business throws receipts into a shoebox. But this company was taking in about $30 million in revenue annually and had the potential to triple sales just to its existing customers. Delivery capacity was getting in the way because expansion would require adding warehouses outfitted with the expensive refrigeration Icy Snacks required. Renting such warehouse space, if it were available, would not be cost-efficient, so the company needed to borrow probably $25 million to buy or build warehouses. You can't ask a bank to underwrite that kind of a loan without records demonstrating your financial performance. The bank needs confidence that the business has managerial practices in place to follow through on its growth plan and a clear view forward showing how the funds will be used and what the impact will be.

How was it possible for a multimillion-dollar company to be stuck in such a dilemma? Icy Snacks had instituted financial management as the need arose. It had a point-of-sale system, a way to route trucks, and inventory controls, but it had no general ledger accounting system. Its tax return preparer relied on bank statements. In other words, it was getting by okay until it needed a big loan. Its product was so good and its salespeople were so talented that the business was running well. But profitability was not meeting potential, so the CEO was leaving money on the table.

The CEO of Icy Snacks was smart to realize she needed help with financial management and strategic planning when she did a few years ago, because the timing helped prevent a potential disaster. John's team helped set up an accounting system over several months and then customized ERP (enterprise resource planning) software.

Around the beginning of 2020, John did a strategic planning exercise with the owners of Icy Snacks by videoconference, at a time when many people hadn't heard of some enterprise tools called Zoom and Google Meet. John suggested they look at what would happen if they had a great year, a good year, or a terrible year ahead. Someone in the meeting mentioned a disease outbreak that had just shut down Wuhan, China. We asked, "Well what if that comes over here? What happens—just worst-case scenario? What if they close everything? What will you have to do?" That question became the basis for the "terrible year" portion of the strategic planning exercise. Of course, it turned out to be work done just in time.

COVID-19 shutdowns of restaurants and other venues with food sales cost Icy Snacks 60 percent of its business almost overnight. Icy Snacks took a page from the book of the strategic plan, enabling it to survive the crisis. The company quickly cut staff and expenses then pivoted within one month to delivering products for other companies to cover its base costs. It actually took over delivering products for competitors that no longer could afford to do it themselves. Soon, it opened three online ventures to diversify its business and regain its retail margins. It positioned itself to emerge from the pandemic with greater sales volume than before.

Functional but Not Systematic

CEOs of a lot of small and medium-sized private companies don't have systems in place to give them a clear view of where their finances stand and what would make them more profitable, or where to save money most effectively in a crisis. It is human nature to want to spend your time and resources on what you are good at. Icy Snacks was good at sales, and it focused on that work rather than financial management or creating a plan to reach the owners' life objectives, including time to do other things they care about. For another CEO whose company's strength is manufacturing, the neglected area might be tracking of sales. I saw that issue at a company that made parts for high-performance vehicles. Business owners' motivations fall into broad categories as we discussed in chapter 1, and some are more driven than others to be 2% CEOs. The Craftspeople type, who have a passion for their product, may also have little interest in looking at financial numbers. They may know that the numbers are important but still shudder at the thought of sitting through a spreadsheet-fueled presentation. They may employ someone to produce financial reports but repeatedly put off meeting with that person. Suddenly, an opportunity comes along to expand into a new market, and the CEO lacks the clarity and confidence to know whether the company has the wherewithal. How many people can it afford to hire? How much office space would it need? Should it buy or lease facilities and equipment? Evaluating options, making what-if budget scenarios, and forecasting revenue and expenses all require being grounded in business basics. When that capability is lacking, it's usually because an entrepreneur was focused elsewhere—on manufacturing, selling, delivering, or otherwise building the business, instead of focusing on overcoming the biggest of its Obstacles to Growth.

> *Evaluating options, making what-if budget scenarios, and forecasting revenue and expenses all require being grounded in business basics.*

The unfortunate result can be sleepless nights for CEOs. They feel the business is getting away from them. It's impossible to lead when you lack confidence in your mastery of your company and clarity about the marketplace. You don't know what you are missing. You don't know what you don't know. In addition, there's the well-known phenomenon of feeling lonely at the top. As Gino Wickman wrote in the best-selling business book *Traction*, "Life is much easier for everyone when you have people around you who genuinely get it, want it, and have the capacity to do it."[6] Even if the CEO has a good leadership team, the person at the top can be isolated from knowledge that subordinates are reluctant to share. The line-of-sight issues discussed in the previous chapter are part of the problem, but growing companies have some other common issues that affect the leader's clarity and confidence.

Role Confusion

Some CEOs make the mistake of lumping together in their minds any employee who prepares reports full of dollar signs. And while bookkeepers, tax preparers, accountants, and controllers have much in common, they all have very different skills. An accountant may be able to fill out a tax form but not be fully aware of all the nuances of tax law compliance. Tax preparers generally stay on top of tax law compliance but are not necessarily skilled or knowledgeable about tax strategy. Controllers run accounting operations such as billing, collections, payroll, and vendor payments.

Specific industries also require different types of expertise that may involve accounting. The telecom industry, for example, has lots of complicated billing transactions and needs specialists to watch for leaking revenue, whether from client churn, fraud, or unreconciled transactions where you can't figure out who should be billed. The more arcane and technical a company's financial management becomes, the more understandable it seems that the CEO ducks out of the conference room when someone pulls up a PowerPoint chart full of numbers.

---

6   Gino Wickman, *Traction: Get a Grip on Your Business* (EOS, 2007).

The company's spreadsheet enthusiasts not only don't speak the CEO's language but inadvertently may come off as not being team players. "If I take an idea to them, they'll tell me all the reasons I can't do it," the CEO is thinking. Steering clear of the number crunchers, the CEO may not realize that those team members have developed overlapping or conflicting roles. Lacking direction, people are predisposed to doing whatever they are most skilled at doing, even if it falls into someone else's job description. Left to their own habits, they play to their own strengths. As a result, at some companies, nobody is performing a necessary financial management function. In such a situation, the CEO may have only a feeling of frustration that something is missing. They are aware that public companies and larger private companies have CFOs but unaware of the role a Growth CFO could perform for them. They may believe their $5 million to $50 million business is not large enough to have the right kind of CFO, and that was partly true before Foresight CFO invented the Growth CFO category.

What's Next?

Some brief introspection is necessary at this point. It would be tempting to jump ahead to what we can do to solve the problems we are discussing. Who wants to dwell on an area of frustration? But we have to make sure we understand what we can control. In financial management, we obviously can't control the economic cycle or extenuating circumstances such as the COVID-19 pandemic, but we can account for them in our planning and have the skills/tools in place to evaluate impact, develop options, and pivot fast with great clarity and confidence. Competitive risks can appear out of nowhere, especially if nobody is in charge of keeping watch on the numbers where they first show up.

CEOS NEED TO ASK THEMSELVES SEVERAL UNCOMFORTABLE QUESTIONS:

1. Is your management team giving you all the information you need to make confident decisions?
2. If not, are they capable of doing so, or do they need help developing those skills?
3. Are there analytical insights that you don't even know?
4. Are you making it easier or harder for them to give you what you need?
5. Do you ever pretend to understand numbers that really make no sense to you?
6. Is your planning oriented toward the status quo?
7. If you are not thinking outside your comfort zone, do you need help being challenged to do so?
8. When you do plan changes, are you and your management team following through?

Some CEOs have a sounding board for admitting when they don't understand what's going on with their budget forecasts and profitability. They may confide in a board member or chief operating officer, or they participate in peer group mastermind sessions. Networking with peers—when it is done for business development, not for recreation—puts you into a learning mindset. So that's an excellent starting point for learning how to obtain necessary financial information in more intuitive ways.

Teaching financial management to nonfinancial managers at Georgetown University made me aware of just how uncomfortable some CEOs and other managers are with numbers. These students were smart, so they were as confused as I was about why they were not seeing what I was seeing on sample balance sheets or cash flow statements. Rather than letting myself get frustrated by their frustration, I decided my job was to figure out a way to teach them to use the numbers. If they had a learning mindset and could avoid pretending to understand when they didn't, they soon were seeing the story behind the numbers.

Competitive risks can appear out of nowhere, especially if nobody is in charge of keeping watch on the numbers where they first show up.

From that story, they could begin to weigh options for action, which put them back into the territory they found comfortable and enjoyable.

CEOs don't have a teacher pushing them to focus on numbers, so how do they get there? The CEOs I meet in my business occasionally have a board or external investors questioning them, and at times they need financial reports to get bank loans. But mostly they are entrepreneurial self-starters who know when to ask for help and are not defensive when their habits of avoiding numbers are challenged by an outside consultant. They might push back, though, if someone suggests they sit down at a specific time just to go over numbers. Often, the entrepreneurial personality is too freewheeling to accept that much structure.

However, the CEO you met in chapter 2, who discovered he had been getting inaccurate financial reports, did agree to monthly meetings to go over numbers once we standardized the reports. The first meeting was rough and took an hour and a half, partly because he didn't want to believe numbers that didn't support what he wanted to do and conflicted with what he called his "experience." We challenged him to show us what was wrong with our data, and he couldn't do so. By the fourth month, we knew we were succeeding in giving the CEO confidence in the process and the numbers because the meeting was down to a half hour. We were having productive conversations about what changed year over year—they sold more to this customer, but they sold less to that customer. This company knew who its biggest customers were, of course, but now it also knew who its best—most profitable—customers were.

Let's Not Waste Time

A CEO who finds excuses to skip meetings about financial performance may have a good reason if those meetings have proven unproductive. Some accountants and controllers have a bad habit of being too comprehensive and talking about numbers that just don't matter. The best practice is to follow the 80/20 principle. As the last chapter noted, that credo holds that roughly 20 percent of customers or 20 percent of marketing efforts generate 80 percent of revenue. Focusing on that 80 percent of revenue, including whatever numbers are involved in producing that value, is key to the critical thinking that leads to good decisions about what actions to take. Naturally, a smart business leader will be annoyed at time spent analyzing numbers irrelevant to the activities most likely to generate the bulk of the company's value.

It's the job of accountants and controllers to keep track of all of a company's activities and transactions continuously. It's the job of the CEO to know the handful that matters most at any given time. It's no wonder they come to meetings with different mindsets. The group dynamics get even more complicated during a financial review session in which managers are trying to avoid accountability or shift blame. Salespeople shade numbers to make their efforts look good. Operations people disown numbers that make them look bad. Managers dismiss variances from the plan as "timing" differences. Allocation of overhead or general costs to different departments can create a lot of internal politics. Going over financial statements that have not been reviewed for accuracy and agreed upon can be a waste of time at best, and at worst toxic blame throwing. A thorough review of the numbers also might be off limits if management has something unsavory to hide.

It may seem efficient to schedule financial reviews less frequently, even just once a year at budget planning time. But lack of exposure to financial reports is a barrier to learning to read them and getting good use of the available data. It's flying blind. A team that reviews and uses numbers monthly develops the skills and information to make longer-term plans. Assuming a CEO is willing to review numbers regularly, financial reports still must be shaped to fit their uses for a particular company. If the reports are too many pages, they may need to be condensed. One tech company CEO we worked with couldn't get into the habit of monthly financial reviews until we brought in an expert in easy-to-understand business intelligence visualizations to make a dashboard he could get excited about.

No Questions? Good! (Or Is It?)

Consistently looking at where you get your money and how you are spending it requires discipline but also a desire to know the answers and compare results to expectations. The story told by the numbers informs decision-making about next steps. The revenue data might not support the CEO's plan for acquiring a new company venue for entertaining clients, which happens to be a boat he's been coveting. Dealing with that kind of disappointment when looking at numbers is preferable to finding out too late that your company has a cash flow problem. Running out of cash when it's time to make payroll is going to run that boat right into a hardship sale. You don't have to love numbers to love knowing your bank balance is sufficient for this month's expenses.

A team that reviews and uses numbers monthly develops the skills and information to make longer-term plans.

Asking questions about revenue and spending can be uncomfortable when a company is burning through cash. Some companies have a verbal tradition, in which executives report their progress without having to back it up with data. Salespeople by nature can tell a good story. They'll come into a meeting and talk about the big contract that is in the pipeline—somewhere. Combine that habit with a CEO who is not comfortable digging into the numbers, and business clarity becomes elusive. Someone in the conference room should be asking the right questions.

No Budget? Big Problem

In a company where decision-making is disciplined by a budget process, managers know whether they have the money to hire someone or not. But when a company is fast growing or dealing with rapid changes in competition or the marketplace, a manager could reasonably ask for special dispensation to go over budget in hiring. Here's the conversation that too often *doesn't* take place because a CEO has a complicated business to run and doesn't have the time or interest to get involved in this level of decision-making:

Manager: I want to hire somebody.

CEO: Tell me why we need them.

Manager: Oh, this guy's skill set is perfect for us. He's a good culture fit, with buzzworthy ideas. He brings a lot to the table.

CEO: No, tell me why we *need* him or any new hire in that position.

Manager: We need to hire this guy, not just anyone, because he has been working for our biggest customer and knows what they want and need. (Not mentioned: this guy is the customer's owner's nephew.)

CEO: How much is it gonna cost?

Manager: Oh, ballpark, I'd guess a hundred grand.

CEO: No, give me an exact number. I want to know if this is an entirely new job or if we are replacing someone. If it's a new job, I want a complete job description and explanation of how that role will help us grow revenue or solve some business problems. If it's a replacement, you need to explain to me why we are paying them more if it's not the same pay as before. Come back when you have the answers.

In small to medium-sized private companies without a CFO, an accountant or controller could be the person questioning the spending. If that person's role is marginalized in decision-making, as often is the case, the business can quickly get into trouble. The next chapter will examine that risk.

CHAPTER 4

THE GROWTH CFO VOID

wouldn't fault a commercial airline pilot for feeling proud, maybe heroic, while sitting in the cockpit, taking responsibility for the safety of hundreds of people. I would be slightly taken aback if the pilot skipped the customary announcement greeting passengers and mentioning the expected time of arrival at the destination. I would be worried if I found out the pilot didn't like looking at the cockpit instruments dashboard and was planning to navigate the old-fashioned way, by looking out the window, as though he were flying a Piper Cub. I would be alarmed if I learned that the controls lacked a working fuel gauge. I would be downright terrified if I discovered the pilot had no flight plan and no navigation system or first officer to help with navigation.

You know where this analogy is headed. Commercial aviation is remarkably safe because airlines have flight planning departments and crews trained to review the plans and monitor instruments that show when adjustments are needed. The CEO of a small, private company is like a pilot in terms of needing a flight plan and navigation help from a copilot and instruments to remain on course. The flight crew, ground crew, mechanics, and air-traffic controllers work like a TrueTEAM to ensure a safe and successful journey, just as a sales team, HR, accounting, and other department managers work together to produce and maintain progress on the company's financial flight plan. The Growth CFO is like a navigator who sits with the pilot on the flight deck throughout the journey, monitoring a financial dashboard. Just as a flight plan ensures there is sufficient fuel, a business budget ensures there is enough cash to arrive at the destination with peace of mind, and maybe a bit early.

Defining the Growth CFO

Any CEO who has a small or medium-sized private company poised to grow or is looking at succession possibilities needs a Growth CFO. This person cannot bring an accountant's mindset to the job, because that mindset is oriented toward compliance, risk reduction, and short-term calculations. A Growth CFO is a planner who thinks in multiyear time frames. A Growth CFO is analytical and asks a lot of questions about objectives and personal motivations. A Growth CFO's goal is to deliver a *wow* factor, not binders or PowerPoints full of comprehensive numbers. At Foresight CFO, we support our Growth CFOs with a unique TrueTEAM approach. The Growth CFO works directly with a CEO but as part of a three-member team. An accounting manager does the legwork on money management and prepares analyses and financial reports. A group lead draws in help from our back office and outside experts as needed, ensuring the Growth CFO is able to fully deliver on the capabilities of our technology and support systems. The Growth CFO marshals and communicates the team's data and expertise.

The TrueTEAM Advantage

Our three-person team is not just a substitute for hiring a full-time CFO. It's a better solution, whether the company is a start-up or mature enough that the owner is planning succession options. A full-time CFO brings the skills and mindset of one person and operates in a certain comfort zone. The TrueTEAM has access to broader skills. Its clarity of purpose from objectives to follow-through is steeped in the experience of a company working with hundreds of CEOs around the world. A full-time CFO works in isolation within one business, while the Growth CFO on the TrueTEAM has access to a continually refined tech platform that provides accountability and professional development. The TrueTEAM uses fintech unavailable to the full-time CFO because the investment wouldn't make sense for one private company.

Some companies have a CFO who is the wrong person for the job. This CFO may be a friend of the CEO, a loyal employee who has been with the company since the beginning, and a hard worker but not the strategic thought partner needed by the CEO of a growing company. I don't want to disparage credentials like being a certified public accountant—I'm a CPA myself—but that training does not prepare anyone to be a Growth CFO. An accountant promoted up the chain to CFO may still be thinking too much in the defensive posture that characterizes a lot of accounting work. That person will diligently point out the risks of any proposed new investments and initiatives but not have the initiative to risk proposing new investments. Very few of these CFOs—actually accountants with a big job title—are forward-looking enough to be thinking about the multiyear journey to an objective. A mindset that values preserving the status quo is not going to be a source of the growth ideas that CEOs want and need to hear.

The ideal Growth CFO has a background running financial planning and analysis (FP&A) for an entrepreneurial company. Experience at a household-name company may look impressive at first glance on a résumé, but at the biggest corporations, deep resources and brand identity go a long way toward making everything work. Someone who directed FP&A at a smaller, private company may be better able to tell you what they actually did to help their organization grow and succeed. Someone who is a controller at one of those companies may aspire to be a CFO, but very few have the right background. They may be too task-oriented because their career has revolved around processing bills, overseeing collections, and making financial reports. Being able to interact with a CEO as a peer and guide the CEO in a variety of circumstances requires substantial business experience and interpersonal communications skills.

It's not easy to find the right talent to fill Growth CFO positions. The one out of 17 Foresight CFO candidates who make it through our application and interview process go through an eight-week impact financial management (IFM) certification program and then start in the second seat with an existing team. Some more experienced people who already are working as CFOs or in financial planning and analysis also come to us for the eight-week program because they want to improve their skills. They don't deliver client services with us but join our Growth CFO TrueTEAM community to continue to sharpen their skills.

Having the wrong person in the CFO job may not be the whole problem when a company has a void that needs to be filled by a Growth CFO. Another factor is role confusion, discussed in the last chapter. Someone at the company, often with the job title controller, must make sure profit and loss are accurately recorded. For example, one company we worked with earned its revenue by getting a small payment each time it processed a transaction, but it relied on outdated and problematic technology. The accounting manager and CFO worked side by side with the company's technology group to make sure a variety of transaction types all were counted and reflected properly in client billing. The more screwed up the technology, the more all-encompassing that controller-type work became. The CFO was acting more like a plumber fixing leaks than what we think of as a Growth CFO. This experience reinforced a lesson I picked up from learning the Who Not How philosophy of renowned business coach Dan Sullivan. He teaches entrepreneurs to stop asking, "How can I do this?" and instead ask, "Who can do this for me?" The right *who* knows *how* to get results.

Huge Opportunity Costs

When a company goes without a Growth CFO, I call it a void because any number of opportunities can disappear into that empty space. Consider a few examples:

- One of the tech giants dangles the prospect of a $100 million buyout before the founder of a start-up then asks to come in and inspect the books. But the books are a mess, and the founder is not sure what opening them up will disclose about the company's value.

- A government contractor's business development chief wants to bid on a huge contract that would require doubling the workforce, but the company can't show that it has the financial strength to get a line of credit or bonded if required.

- A company's revenue chart looks like a black diamond ski slope, and the CEO is asking for ideas to reverse the slide.

The managers look down and pretend to take notes, but the conference room is eerily silent.

Growth CFOs' contributions quickly pay for themselves. We will show in chapter 8 how significant cost savings often emerge in just the first few weeks of a TrueTEAM approach in which a Growth CFO leads a financial health check. CEOs who think of a Growth CFO as a cost of doing business, like accounting or tax preparation, often delay or miss this opportunity.

Avoiding Leaps of Faith

When the CEO asks for advice on ways forward, the Growth CFO's hands-on work is to narrow down and analyze the options. How do they compare to each other and to the status quo? How much would we have to spend? Month to month, how will money come in and go out? When will the break-even point happen? If we cannot afford to chase after an opportunity, is there an option to take a smaller step toward it first? What would that step-up approach look like? Answering all these questions saves the CEO from having to make intuitive decisions in an information void.

A Growth CFO must analyze the entire business to see which parts might be holding the company back. It's not enough to just oversee the financial management. Having some project management skills enables the Growth CFO to evaluate whether an initiative is being planned properly, with the right team in place and a realistic timeline. When the company is evaluating how much it should spend on new lead generation software, the Growth CFO doesn't need to be an expert in that area to get involved by asking basic questions. What are the software's key attributes, and how do they matter to our operations? How do we know it will meet our needs? How many options were considered, and how rigorously were they tested against each other? The point is not to discourage spending money but to lead the way to spending money properly. In the case of a company with outdated technology, the path to growth may require spending more rather than hobbling operations with cheap workarounds and stifling profitability.

A Growth CFO doesn't magically produce solutions to longstanding problems. But asking the right questions can reveal solutions that were over-

> *The point is not to discourage spending money but to lead the way to spending money properly.*

looked or disregarded. It can open the CEO to seeing gaps in staff capabilities and options such as bringing in outside expertise.

Do It Yourself?

We all know how do-it-yourself projects can end up costing more money than hiring an expert to start with. A CEO without a Growth CFO must fill that role sometimes in key situations such as finding and negotiating a large loan. That route is another missed opportunity because when a CFO negotiates the loan terms, narrowing down possibilities to just a few options, they can bring in the CEO to finalize the deal and make additional last-minute requests of the lender. The lender almost always grants some additional consideration. Just as important, the CEO doesn't burn up valuable time shopping for and negotiating the loan. The same logic applies to negotiations to attract private investors or to sell the business.

If there is no Growth CFO, then the CEO either is their own growth CFO or else has none. Those are pretty much the only alternatives. The CEO is either getting it done, or it's not getting done. Without a Growth CFO, a CEO is likely to feel exhausted—constantly running a marathon instead of just running the last mile of a relay race. Unless the CEO happens to have all the skills of a Growth CFO, which is rarely the case, the CEO trying to take on that role is another instance of having the wrong person in the job.

DOES A CPA NEED A GROWTH CFO?

Owners of private accounting firms are worrying a lot about their future these days. Technology has automated much of their work, as anyone who has used software to prepare a tax return can easily envision. Rapid advances in artificial intelligence could further erode the market for accounting services. A CPA firm is a good candidate for a Growth CFO not to outsource accounting work but to guide it to a future in which it has a culture of impact and innovation. The culture of accounting firms centers on compliance, which makes it difficult for them to see opportunities to break out of the strictures of a declining market.

One big opportunity described well in an October 2021 commentary in *Accounting Today*[7] is to offer advisory services. It's a difficult pivot for several reasons. Our experience is that accountants do not see themselves as advisors, and if they take on the role of giving business advice, they will need training and guidance to structure the service, sell its value to clients, and determine pricing. There isn't a boiler-

---

7   Jody Padar, "How to Shift to Advisory Services," *Accounting Today*, October 12, 2021, https://www.accountingtoday.com/opinion/how-to-shift-to-advisory-services.

plate approach. Each firm must devise a plan appropriate to the confidence levels and skills of its people, the needs of its clients, and the time the firm is willing to devote. Financial planning and analysis are different types of work than being a controller, accountant, or auditor, and developing new skills takes time and training. The Growth CFO is skilled at helping CPA firm partners cross this chasm.

Avoiding the Fixed Mindset

Mindset is as important as skills in qualifying someone to be an effective Growth CFO. If you are a CEO who has been convinced that you need a Growth CFO, you may be tempted to start by looking internally at your controller or accounting manager. Does that person have the skills and mindset to question colleagues and the boss about their objectives, their personal motivation, and their spending plans? The most common thing we see that gets in the way of success for a CFO who is promoted within the ranks is a fixed mindset, a desire to hold on to the status quo. Think back on the sudden business

Without a Growth CFO, a CEO is likely to feel exhausted—constantly running a marathon instead of just running the last mile of a relay race.

impact of the COVID-19 pandemic, which forced businesses to rapidly change policies, procedures, and strategies. Did your prospective Growth CFO formulate and lead at least some of the changes in order to preserve or grow the business? Did you find yourself saying, "That's a great idea! Why didn't we think of that before?"

People with a fixed mindset tend to have a ready excuse for not questioning the status quo: it's not their job. They might not resist an initiative but also don't get behind it. They don't have the big picture in their mind of the whole business, even if they have been there from the start. They don't really keep up with changes affecting their company in the marketplace or business environment outside of their immediate area of job responsibilities. They are not going to be proactive in bringing up growth opportunities to the CEO.

The fixed mindset presents long-term risks beyond missed opportunities, such as developing new products and services or new markets for existing products and services. The desire to hold on to the status quo is an obstacle to succession planning, a big issue in small and medium-sized private companies. Whatever the CEO has in mind—passing the torch, selling the business, or closing it entirely—planning years in advance will improve the outcome for everyone involved. The reasons will be explained in chapter 7—of this book, that is. Hopefully we're not talking about chapter 7 bankruptcy!

Attaining Multiyear Foresight

Some CEOs have been lulled into thinking their financial planning is adequate. They have a CFO, controller, or someone with a different job title overseeing the budget and cash management, closing the books each year, and dealing with audits and tax compliance. When called upon to evaluate a new project, this finance person can provide some analysis. The perspective stops there.

Dropping a financial report onto the desk of a manager each month is not the same as helping that manager understand and make good use of the numbers. Department managers and CEOs tend to be absorbed with their present challenges. A CFO who can help them get their annual budget right is a blessing, even when it's not received that way. The next step up for strategic planning is being able to see two or three years ahead. A reasonably accurate multiyear perspective allows the CEO to have very different business conversations with internal and external stakeholders when it comes to raising capital for strategic growth. It also helps in negotiating with suppliers and attracting top talent.

Missed opportunities are not obvious without doing the work to plan for them and evaluate options. For example, maybe you don't see your business as being able to acquire other companies. But what if buying another company would be the most effective way for you to grow, versus adding products, services, and capacity internally? Should you be building up a cash reserve to seize such an acquisition opportunity? Do you have financial performance data to make a case for borrowing the money? A Growth CFO is not necessarily someone who has all the answers but someone who is willing to do the work to identify and open up options for a CEO, working side by side.

The Growth CFO to the Rescue

When a company is in trouble, burning cash, a CEO will naturally grow anxious, but an effective Growth CFO will remain calm. When you are flying an airplane, and an alarm sounds and warning lights flash on the flight deck, you can't panic if you want to survive the emergency.

A CEO can be very hardworking and responsive to problems but still feel frazzled or stuck in a rut because of inadequate financial management. Let's look at the example of Ernest Robinson, a CEO in his fifties who gets up before dawn and works long days running a B2B service provider. Robinson swoops in and out a lot, sometimes griping over some small thing. His corporation's outdated technology results in a lot of little crises to respond to and a lot of blame being thrown around. He has hired smart people for his management team but trained them to be wingmen, not leaders. They bring problems, not solutions, to his attention, and they wait for him to tell them what to do. Then he swoops in and makes everything more complicated than it needs to be.

When it comes time to look at numbers, Robinson wants to see the revenue and expenses down to the penny, by vendor, by week. The complexity he demands requires a process that cannot be automated, so it makes for a lot of extra work. The company's financial managers are confused about their roles and the point of their work. One day after a fairly short time at the company, the accounting manager gets fed up with the toxic environment and decides to move on. She calls the CFO, who has been functioning more as an accounting control-ler himself, to give her two-week notice. "What a coincidence," the CFO replies. "I just quit yesterday." Unable to build and empower a real executive team, Robinson is flying blind just as much as those CEOs we described in the last chapter who shy away from looking at numbers. He is a serial entrepreneur who is starting to get unsolicited buyout offers, but he has no convincing way to know or show what his company is worth.

This is the point where you may be expecting me to tell you how a Growth CFO rescued Robinson. I'm going to introduce a plot twist into this fictionalized story: Robinson brought in a Growth CFO from my company who developed a budget process and management structure to provide more confidence for decision-making. Depart-ment managers began to take financial responsibility for their part of the business, which remained profitable. But the company didn't fully improve its technology. Its services became commoditized in a maturing industry, and nobody was leading the way to spend properly on innovation because Robinson never resolved the role confusion between the controller and the CFO, expecting one person to do both jobs. That impossible expectation created a lost opportunity for growth that could have amounted to tens of millions of dollars.

We have dwelled a lot in the first part of this book on the obstacles, risks, and warning signs the CEO of a small or medium-sized private business is likely to encounter. As a business grows increasingly complex, problems crop up outside the CEO's line of sight. Maintaining clarity and confidence becomes difficult. CEOs usually are not oriented toward digging into financial data to find answers and options. The numbers-savvy people in the organization are often incapable of helping and may seem like more of a liability than an asset. But when properly done, financial management provides ways to obliterate obstacles, control risks, and respond appropriately to warning signs. The rest of the book explains how to benefit from good financial management by partnering with a Growth CFO.

The process doesn't work equally well for all kinds of CEOs. It requires introspection and an open, learning mindset. It begins with a desire to eliminate blind spots and pursue objectives, as we will discuss in the next chapter. We also will look at why and how a business might unleash exponential growth by not playing along with what generally works in its industry.

CHAPTER 5

OBLITERATE THE OBSTACLES TO GROWTH

I f you had to make up a description of a company poised for growth, you might come up with something like one of our first Growth CFO clients, which I'll call Tsawesome Corp. The technology company found itself in the awesome situation of specializing in a type of software that was becoming more popular and essential every day. The company had leading-edge thinkers, valuable intellectual property, and a product that was a time saver for a lot of business customers. Tsawesome's CEO's goal was to grow the company enough to catch the notice of suitors for an acquisition, and that strategy required spending a lot of money. We helped set up a growth plan and a budget, but the spending got ahead of the cash flow, and one day Tsawesome ran out of cash.

Of course, the story doesn't end there. We just needed to figure out what went wrong and fix it. The problem turned out to involve talent management—too many highly paid software engineers not given enough new projects that would generate revenue through billable hours. We addressed that issue, improved the sales pipeline and tightly matched it to the hiring cycle, and focused on key performance indicators. As a result, Tsawesome Corp.'s run rate—the financial performance measure that a suitor would use to predict its future performance—became very impressive. The strategic buyout the CEO had hoped for happened a year sooner than expected. Tsawesome lives on as a kind of skunk works inside a larger computer technology company.

In chapter 2, we compared the CEO running a fast-growing start-up to a pilot who had gone from flying a Piper Cub to a jetliner—no longer able to navigate by looking out the windshield. Tsawesome had become that jetliner, and its pilot needed to stay on top of a lot of switches, dials, and dashboard knobs to adjust the flight path. Mistakenly going too high or too low wouldn't necessarily result in a crash if the pilot knew how to use the controls to respond properly.

The Financial Controls

If you are not a properly qualified CFO, you may find the financials generated by accounting systems as baffling as jetliner cockpit controls would appear to someone who is not a properly trained pilot. The very smart, technically savvy people running Tsawesome Corp. realized they needed to outsource the CFO role because they were not getting the data they needed from their financial controls or accounting operation. What they had was a compliance chart of accounts. They could look at a dashboard and see where their software was installed, how many licenses they had sold, to which customers, and for how much money. But when it came to planning, the CEO didn't really know whether the company could afford the initiatives that would help it grow. We came in and reorganized their accounting system to measure performance per line of business. A performance accounting system shows the CEO the profitability of each type of goods or services a company is providing and each project it takes on. Then we worked side by side with profit center managers, showing them how to interpret and apply the numbers.

A company needs to know how much money it has in the bank and whether it made or lost money by the end of the tax year, but that's not enough data for growth and succession planning. Tsawesome Corp. went from knowing how much money it had to knowing exactly what brought in that money. The accounting system showed net profit per project because revenue per project was tied to cost per project and to the business units involved. The CEO could get a profit and loss, or P&L, report for every activity, which obviously was eye opening and crucial information for a company that had experienced a cash crunch. A few years later, when the acquisition offers started coming in, the CEO could evaluate them based not on instinct but on real financial trend data.

To What End?

"Start with the end in mind," Stephen R. Covey wrote in his business best seller *The 7 Habits of Highly Effective People.* In developing a habit of reviewing financial reports, the end to have in mind is clarity and confidence for reaching the CEO's business and personal objectives. The prerequisite is being clear on what those goals are. In the daily grind, it's possible to lose sight of why you are in the business and what you care about. We always ask these questions before we start devising the financial flight plan, as you will see in the upcoming chapters.

It gets personal. In one memorable case, when I asked a CEO the key question, "Why is this outcome important to you?" the answer had to do with his upbringing. His family suffered because his father was a business owner who really hated going to work every day. This CEO was able to confide, because we had built up that kind of relationship, that his motivation was to have a company where people were healthy and happy and to have a life experience different from the miserable one his father had endured.

Getting an early start on succession planning, we ask CEOs, "What do you really want in your life? Do you want to be able to step back from working in the business? Do you want to be able to travel and see your children or grandchildren?" These questions help us understand the motivations we discussed in chapter 1, such as who wants to be a 2% CEO and who is a Freedom Fighter type. CEOs also confide in us about what they need right now for household income— or what their spouses tell them they need. Some have not been able to pull much money out of the business, and they need to start doing so to care for aging parents or other dependents, send kids to college, or save for retirement. Some want to make as much money for as long as possible because they have goals involving leaving a legacy through inheritance or bequests. The Mountain Climber types may envision having a building at a college or medical center named after them.

CEOs unfortunately often do not have someone willing and able to explore with them how their personal and business objectives are aligned. They need an objective person whom they trust and can talk to about their worries. That person must be able to warn them about blind spots, given the line-of-sight issues that we discussed in chapter 2. They don't need a yes-person. They need someone who will be direct with them and who also is knowledgeable about their business, its resources, its market, and its finances. Some CEOs who feel alone and isolated will turn to a consultant or hire someone very experienced to take on an interim role in the C-suite. Our concept of outsourcing to a Growth CFO is a smarter approach because the CEO will have a TrueTEAM alongside for the full journey. As you will see in the chapters ahead, the team will have skills and capabilities far beyond what that one interim executive can bring.

Some readers may be thinking, "I have a team. I couldn't have built my business without one." My experience is that some CEOs fail to share their personal objectives with their team until prompted to do so by my questions. At the meeting in which the CEO confided the story about his father, a stunned member of his team blurted out, "We worked with you for 12 years and didn't know that's what you wanted!"

Without setting goals and objectives first, it is hard to see what actions to prioritize to overcome obstacles. As Growth CFOs, we do a lot of backstage work that we will discuss in the next chapter to make sure CEOs are getting good numbers. On the front stage, we speak weekly with CEOs about the decisions, planning, and follow-through needed to achieve their primary objectives. Those discussions focus on what it will take to obliterate their specific Obstacles to Growth, whether it involves winning new customers, keeping and growing existing customers, proactively getting access to capital, or ensuring they have the right people and capacity to improve financial performance.

Performing 80/20 Analysis

A ratio that is easy to understand, even for the most math-challenged among us, is the 80/20 principle we have mentioned in chapters 2 and 3. Intuitively, it makes sense to spend most of your time and financial resources on whatever gives you the most value. That's why I spend the bulk of my waking hours either working or caring for myself and my family, and why I pay others to mow my lawn and change the oil in my car. Yet we find businesses pouring time and resources into things that have little value. For example, we analyzed an inside sales call center to see how efficient it was at getting customers on board, versus signing themselves up online. We found the additional step of calling interrupted enrollment more so than it smoothed the process. Basically, the company was spending a lot of money talking to reluctant prospects. Changes made based on the 80/20 analysis resulted in reducing labor costs by 73 percent and increasing profit by over a million dollars. The business invested in improving its web-based technology and streamlining customer acquisition. Customer conversion rates eventually increased by 18 percent, bringing in $18 million in additional revenue and $3.6 million in annual profit.

When we look at a company's costs of doing business, there may be 20 to 30 line items, but typically just a few make up 80 percent of the costs. Effectively managing those few big cost centers is more efficient than chasing them all. For one of our clients, labor was 85 percent of its costs. We set up policies and procedures to monitor hourly and contract labor doing fieldwork to see where cost overruns were occurring compared to preapproved levels. Once managers started keeping score weekly and monthly, they could adjust targets and operations proactively. It was easy to identify team members who were not pulling their weight—the bottom 20 percent. Managers retrained or worked closely with this group then cut those who did not get on track. The result was turning seven-figure losses into seven-figure gains.

Finding the Way to Bold Moves

Business owners often tell us they want to double their business in five years. The subtext is that they are presenting an ambitious objective as a challenge to us: "How are you going to help us get *there*? We do some back-of-the-envelope math and tell them that at current interest rates, 100 percent growth in five years is only 15 percent per year, and they could set their sights a lot higher. (If you want to know more about the math involved, look up "the rule of 72.") By focusing on the obstacles that they would have to overcome (winning new customers, proactive access to capital, and the others we discussed in chapter 1), they get clarity about their options. Bold moves that might have seemed unthinkable emerge as possibilities. Sometimes you read about a business achieving 1,000 percent growth in five years, usually connected with a story about that company's norm-shattering approach. Business media and books are full of stories about entrepreneurs who dared to be different, some becoming household names like Jeff Bezos, Sir Richard Branson, Steve Jobs, and Elon Musk.

The stories about business legends make it easy to confuse the innovative routes they have taken with risk taking or marketing prowess. The stories gloss over how bold successes usually begin with careful research, planning, and analysis that account for or minimize risks. Branson started Virgin Atlantic Airways with one leased jetliner—and if the service had fizzled, the lease had a one-year escape clause. Nobody would ever describe Musk's self-promotion as traditional marketing. Small and medium-sized private businesses will never have the free advertising Musk gets with his enormous social media following, but they often get free promotion in the media and by word of mouth when they do something out of the ordinary. As I write this, the business press is churning out stories about bold moves companies are taking during the post-COVID-19 economic recovery. Three private companies commercialized space flight. A hamburger franchise is offering a $1,500 sign-on bonus to cope with a labor shortage. A tech company is closing for a week of paid time off to alleviate employee burnout. A mobile phone service is offering a new smartphone every two years. Companies are embracing a virtual technology–enabled work environment. People are using their private vehicles for delivery and transportation services. A Florida business tried to retain skilled workers with a drawing for two brand new and mortgage-free houses. Bold moves like those can simply involve keeping employees happy. As the best-selling business book author Tom Peters famously said, "Your customer is never happier than your employees."

Playing along with industry norms, chasing the same customers or clients as your competitors, and hitting the same price points can produce linear growth. Hermann Simon, a leading expert on pricing strategy, invoked a Russian proverb in writing about how to maximize value through pricing: "In every market, there are two kinds of fools. One charges too much, the other charges too little." Prices determine how much money you make. In my experience, most small private businesses undercharge because the owner is price sensitive, wanting to win every possible client or customer instead of establishing value. Value pricing is tough, but it is worth the effort.

If you want exponential growth, you may have to boldly attract a specific market by positioning your company with a unique sales proposition. Repositioning can necessitate cutting or raising prices, something that obviously should be done only after the type of careful financial planning work our Growth CFOs perform. That groundwork on overcoming obstacles also should precede any restructuring of business processes—as Tsawesome Corp. did when it fixed its problem with having highly paid engineers sitting idle.

In sum, bold moves can involve five Ps: people, positioning, promotion, process, and pricing. But if you expect that sixth P, profits, to result, don't leap into anything without studying your marketplace and doing some critical thinking about overcoming obstacles and about all possible outcomes. An offbeat idea that worked great for some other business could put yours in peril.

Unleashing Growth

Let's return to where we began this chapter, with a CEO willing to spend a lot of money toward a goal of growing the business enough to catch the notice of suitors for an acquisition. A Growth CFO, coming in from outside, asked what made Tsawesome Corp. unique. What did its clients and customer really care about? From that starting point, we performed an exercise to identify the best areas of growth potential. Should the company put its efforts into existing products or new products? Should it focus on existing customers or new customers? Should it be trying to sell new products to existing customers or existing products to new customers? That conversation was exhilarating because of all the possibilities, but also because the company executives finally had an objective way to assess options against each other. They could see which ideas were more affordable and potentially profitable.

Bold moves can involve five Ps: people, positioning, promotion, process, and pricing.

The alternative approach for too many businesses is chasing growth through ad hoc decision-making. Personalities come into play. Is the CEO a risk taker by nature? Is the executive pushing the idea the CEO's favorite, or a skillful salesperson? Risks and costs are overlooked because an executive is allowed to pitch the idea without attaching a budget. Doubters are afraid to speak up because everyone has gotten so excited. Nobody is forecasting long-term costs and break-even points. People who have been successful in the past relying on their gut instincts do so one time too often. Their plans are undone because they had a blind spot. Who hasn't heard of a tech start-up that failed because the brilliant kids running it became too enamored with their product to pay attention to whether it would ever turn a profit?

The bold moves that emerge from focusing on overcoming Obstacles to Growth are performed with clarity and confidence because they start with objectives in mind and are grounded in sound financial management practices. A Growth CFO TrueTEAM approach develops the abilities of managers to look at fundamental financial reports every month with weekly dashboards to take proactive action. Focusing on accounting and budgeting may be the last thing they want to do, but it gradually feels more natural as it empowers them to take ownership of their P&L and make better decisions. A $10 million company can have the objective of growing tenfold and what skeptics consider a crazy idea for getting there, but the path to that goal must be realistic—developed and customized for that unique business—with adequate planning and follow-through. The process can be liberating for managers and for CEOs, who gain peace of mind or see a way out if they're trying to exit the business. I have seen great outcomes result for some business owners, but only for those willing to commit time and effort to developing certain habits. Those Habits of Profitability are the subject of the next chapter.

CHAPTER 6

ESTABLISH THE FIVE HABITS OF PROFITABILITY

The inventor of the hottest new home appliance had teamed up with an experienced offshore manufacturing firm to get the company WishfulWand in business at a scale where it could supply major US retailers. A sales consultant who lined up the first big retail contract mentioned, almost in passing, that the company should be prepared to supply millions of units. If consumer demand stayed strong, and the supply lagged far behind, interest in the product would vanish. Retailers would not commit to orders that could not be delivered in a timely way.

The CEO of WishfulWand had a good track record in his prior business, marketing a home appliance that was very profitable until cheap knockoffs that were sold online commoditized the market. Luckily, an unexpected buyout offer allowed him to sell that prior business right before the bottom dropped out. He had adequate capital for his start-up and a line of credit available for WishfulWand to grow. The bank had required a lot of documentation, including a detailed sales forecast. Based on the consultant's optimistic comments and his own instincts, he had forecast selling five million units in the first year.

That sales forecast took on a life of its own as the company got established. WishfulWand started hiring staff for any work it could not outsource. It contracted with a professional employer organization to handle payroll and benefits but kept sales, marketing, and inventory and facilities management in house. Office space, warehouses, and trucks were all leased at first, but once the company seemed firmly established, managers recommended buying warehouses and trucks as more cost-efficient. The advice made sense, because WishfulWand didn't want to get caught with shiploads of product coming in and inadequate storage and distribution capacity.

Gradually, though, the facilities managers started mentioning problems with the warehouses filling up and trucks sitting idle. These warnings didn't make sense to the CEO because the sales managers had consistently reported lots of big contracts with major retailers in the pipeline. Since it was almost time to go back to the bank for more credit, the CEO finally ordered up a detailed financial report. His staff had to contract out the forensic accounting work to get it done, because the company had no organized system to track revenue or spending details. The CEO could see the lump sums going in and out of the checking account, but he had no idea whether the cash balance would cover accrued expenses. He didn't really know whether his business was making a profit or, if not, how far in the future it might reach the break-even point.

You probably know where this fictitious but all-too-realistic story is leading. The sales forecasts of a lot of companies are aspirational, especially if they are new at financial planning. It is very easy for them to overauthorize new hires and buy too much equipment and inventory. If they are smart enough to get regular, detailed financial reports, they can make course corrections based on actual sales. In the case of WishfulWand, we'll say sales fell 25 percent below expectations. The CEO immediately froze new hiring and backed out of pending truck and warehouse purchases to shore up the numbers for his company's next line of credit application.

No Taste for Accounting

One thing we never hear a business owner say is, "I started this company to have a great accounting operation." People who start a business know they'll have to pay taxes, so they hire a tax preparer and an accountant to keep the books, but those are the last people they think about and value. Most CEOs don't like to look at numbers and are focused on developing their products or sales. The businesses may grow substantially with the owners winging it when it comes to the numbers that would show how they are performing financially. Consequently, they don't have a firm handle on their revenue or costs by client, by product line, or by service line. If that seems like a stupid way to run a business, that's because it is. I'm not sorry to say so, because I have seen what happens when managers are given good numbers.

Once a company gets its managers looking at fundamental financial reports every month, the numbers gradually start to make sense and the executives make better decisions. The entire company culture evolves from one grounded in fear to one with a learning mindset. Eventually, the business leaders don't remember or don't want to think about what it was like flying the plane by the seat of their pants before they learned how to read the cockpit dashboard dials.

Surprises, both pleasant and unpleasant, will emerge from the numbers. Business leaders may realize they can afford to start an exciting initiative they were putting off. Or they may discover that bad spending decisions were made. In the absence of regular financial reviews, managers offer salaries or sign contracts that are out of line with norms in their industry or even their own company. Seeing how that salary fits into the overall personnel budget or how that contract affects the P&L can prevent bad decisions from being made in isolation.

Regular reviews of financial data also can help prevent a company from getting stuck in a shrinking comfort zone. Products and services can become commoditized and less profitable over time, especially when sales managers give discounts to get orders instead of establishing value. Business owners who see their margins shrinking may realize they need to shift away from parts of the business their people are comfortable with and into something more cutting edge. Change can be difficult and awkward. Not everyone wants to admit that what worked yesterday doesn't work anymore, and the people in the company with innovative ideas may be outside the CEO's orbit. By asking line managers and salespeople questions about revenue and other financial numbers, a Growth CFO can not only issue a wake-up call about the need to change but also make sure ideas reach the CEO. We don't have all the answers, just a rational way of analyzing what options are the best ones.

Making a Workout Routine

In chapter 3, we discussed the dangers of making leaps of faith in a business by not having what we call a Growth CFO to oversee financial management. In the case of WishfulWand, the Growth CFO void resulted in overspending. For other companies, failing to look at their numbers can result in missed opportunities. They win contracts they must defer or cancel because they don't have the people or resources to do the work. Or they hire too many people for a product or service that lacks market value and end up burning their profits and laying off those people. Or they can't get a line of credit to cover timing differences or can't get through bonding underwriting if that's required.

> *We don't have all the answers, just a rational way of analyzing what options are the best ones.*

In this chapter, I want to make clear that the Growth CFO solution involves a lot more than bringing in an outsider gifted at asking difficult questions and doing math. The solution is a team effort in which managers throughout the business participate. We train the managers in skills with numbers that give them clarity and confidence to act. The habits the managers develop in the process take the weight off the CEO's shoulders.

We trademarked the FIVE Habits of Profitability as a relatable name for crucial and rewarding work that many CEOs initially are reluctant to take on. Consistently reviewing financial reports every month is a fitness habit. Like going to the gym, it's not easy the first time you do it. You may feel intimidated, uncomfortable, and uncertain whether you are doing things right. Executives who haven't previously taken ownership of their financial results may feel like they are naked in a crowd. But once going to the gym—I mean going to the monthly financial review—becomes an established habit, feelings change. You may look forward to each session, especially if you are getting positive feedback from improving results.

When results are not what you hoped for, when you are over budget or have not met the plan's goals, the financial review is even more worth the time spent. If the reason for the variance is not obvious (for example, COVID-19 shut down your business or it suffered from the 2021 Great Resignation), the numbers help you figure out what happened or what actions to take. Managers and team members may not all agree on strategy, but at least they are looking at the same scoreboard. Within three to six months of developing the habit of monthly reviews, the benefits become obvious, even to the skeptics.

The FIVE Habits

I have spoken in many seminars and workshops in recent years about these FIVE Habits, adapting the finer points to different situations and audiences. This is an overview of generally applicable recommendations:

HABIT 1—ACHIEVE POSITIVE CASH FLOW

Recommendations we make about managing cash are always customized because needs vary so much among businesses. Some industries build up a lot of cash, others fly close to the trees. For a loose guideline, you could add up your current liabilities, including your accounts payable, recurring bills, and payroll, and multiply by two for a decent cash threshold. If you regularly have only enough cash to pay your bills, you might be kept up at night stressing over whether you can make payroll. If you are cutting it closer than industry peers, you may need to be more disciplined.

A good first step is making a 12-week cash forecast, essentially listing every payment you expect to come in and go out. If you know more is going out than coming in, you can start doing something about it. You can put off expenses, and to some extent you can control the payment of invoices. Obviously, if you don't pay your rent and utility bills, at some point you'll come in and find the doors are locked and the electricity has been shut off. You don't want to miss your payroll deadline either. But maybe your accountant is paying some other bills too promptly and can give you a little more cash leeway without alienating any of your vendors.

Sometimes the cash problems are too deep to be fixed with controls on the timing of your spending. Businesses get creative figuring out how to reserve some cash. They sell prepaid subscriptions or offer discounts to those who pay in advance. Paying bills up to a month after receiving the service—or receiving the invoice—has a long history that's hard to reverse. But any business will be better off if it can tweak cash flow in its favor, even in limited ways, to avoid the cost of borrowing money.

We help our clients move to a positive cash flow with a financial management tool called the cash conversion cycle. In simple terms, we are measuring how long it takes them to bill and get paid, so they know how much cash they need. For example, a government contractor may have no choice but to wait up to 90 days to get paid, going through three months of payroll uncompensated for the work performed. Since they can't make the government speed up its bureaucracy, they must have either cash reserves, a line of credit, or other access to capital.

SAVE THIS THOUGHT

Beyond the reassurance of knowing you can pay your bills, a cash reserve provides the following:

- A cushion against economic downturns, natural disasters, and shocks like war, terrorism, and pandemics
- An ability to take advantage of sudden opportunities, such as an acquisition

---

Similarly, in a manufacturing industry relying on raw materials shipped from overseas, there will be a long cycle between ordering those materials and having the product produced, shipped, received, and sold. Vendors in that industry may accept slower payment than, for example, vendors of a cloud software company that gets an instant credit card payment for an upcoming year of service. But that software company may have had to invest heavily in servers and pay skilled programmers for months before those expenses paid off in product sales.

Sometimes, owners of small, privately held businesses can't get a line of credit without a personal guarantee. They don't want to have their personal credit score remain burdened for years by such a large debt, or maybe even put up their home as loan collateral. We work with them to show lenders the business can carry the line of credit without the personal guarantee, or we help them look elsewhere for capital.

WHERE DID THE MONEY GO?

After a company has been around for a while, it should be good at pricing its goods and services, but that's not the case for companies that don't regularly review financial numbers. They fail to notice direct costs are going up each year while they are keeping prices fixed and their profit margins are shrinking. That's when we see well-established companies come up short on cash.

HABIT 2—DRIVE IMPACT WITH THE FINANCIAL SCOREBOARD

If a meeting to review monthly financial reports is dominated by a CFO reading numbers off a chart, it's a terrible meeting, no matter how accurate those numbers are. By good numbers, we mean ones that managers take ownership of and understand as both accurate and meaningful to them. Habit 2 begins with teaching managers to use the numbers like a scoreboard, apply critical thinking to those numbers, and act or propose actions based on financial performance data.

WHY CALL IT A SCOREBOARD?

Imagine watching a baseball game without a scoreboard. It's a long game. You get up to get a snack and again to use the bathroom. It's so convenient having the stats on display when you come back to make sure you know how your team is doing. In a company, we hope everybody is on the same team, so we are not looking for a score to decide a winner or a loser. But we can look to the scoreboard to see when we need to change strategy, when it's time to bunt, and when it's time to swing for the fences.

Before the meeting, managers should read through the transaction details they are responsible for and flag anything they don't recognize, so whoever is doing the accounting can resolve mistakes. This quality control takes about 30 minutes and keeps the meeting on track. The manager should be able to explain in the meeting why numbers are above or below expectations and propose actions in response without setting off a time-wasting debate about whether the numbers are accurate or significant.

The best outcome that can result from giving managers a clear view of the financial consequences of their actions is that they take extreme ownership over the P&L in their areas of responsibility. At first, they see the financial reports only as backward looking. But with the right training, they can develop the skill to use the numbers to look forward, plan realistic budgets, and engineer profitability into their operations. Once they have a baseline understanding of their P&L, they can do the fun part of budgeting, which is running "what if" scenarios to engineer revenue and profit: "What if we launch a new product?" and "What if we stop offering this service?"

All too many small and medium-sized private companies engage in a lot of impulsive decision-making and guesswork because they never implement formal budget processes. They know they should have a budget, and they should reforecast that budget as the year goes on and unexpected changes affect their P&L. They just never get around to learning that skill or doing that work. Fear is a big reason. Managers will say something like, "Gosh, I don't know what's gonna happen six months from now. How can I possibly budget for it?" They fear being held accountable for something they don't control.

Attitudes are different after monthly financial reviews become a habit. Managers who have taken ownership of their P&L feel more comfortable with a budget than they would without one. If asked to make a change or try something new, they might reply, "I can't make a decision until I look at my numbers." Having managers internalize the skill of engineering profitability into what they do is liberating for them but also for a CEO, who can now

- gain peace of mind, knowing that decisions are in good hands;

- achieve annual objectives;

- have the financial resources to do what they want, when they want;

- think about taking a vacation without her cell phone;

- retire from the role but still have a hand in the business;

- retire from the business to do other kinds of work; or

- sell the company.

Some companies will build dashboards of key performance indicators (KPIs) to track their sales or operations in real time, or weekly. A company may track its P&L monthly and track some nonfinancial numbers on a different schedule. How many calls is a salesperson making each day? How many marketing emails are opened each week? How many new clients is a professional firm taking on each quarter? These KPIs are good numbers if they give managers information that they need to make course corrections as needed.

ACTIONABLE NUMBERS

A leading indicator is a measurement that helps a business predict outcomes. Counting potential new clients in our pipeline helps my business predict its future revenue. Measurements can be financial or nonfinancial. A restaurant can measure the average dollar amount of diners' checks, track what food it is wasting, and time the average turnover of its tables. KPIs should cover all functions and departments of a business, and they should be actionable. If the average time it takes a company to fill a position is a key driver of profitability, that time spent getting skilled labor on board is an actionable KPI. The company may need to spend more on retention, training, or recruiting.

Some companies are very proud of their net promoter score, which is based on a simple survey question asking how likely the respondent is to recommend the company to a friend or colleague. That measurement is a good conversation starter for planning strategy, but it's not an actionable KPI because it is not tied to a specific activity. Collectively, the company has too many detractors and not enough advocates, so now what? Should it teach its employees to smile more? Even if the survey question is applied to a specific product or service, what's working or not working?

HABIT 3—DEVELOP THE EIGHT
DRIVERS TO GET PAID TWICE

Sometimes a CEO needs to step back from the day-to-day concerns and ask, "Where am I going on the journey with my business?"—a journey from founding the business to the seven succession options that we will be discussing in the next chapter. We have developed a tool at Foresight CFO to help with that question. Borrowing from John Warrillow's 2011 book *Built to Sell*, it involves eight drivers—or qualities in a business that enhance or limit its value.

The Eight Performance Drivers

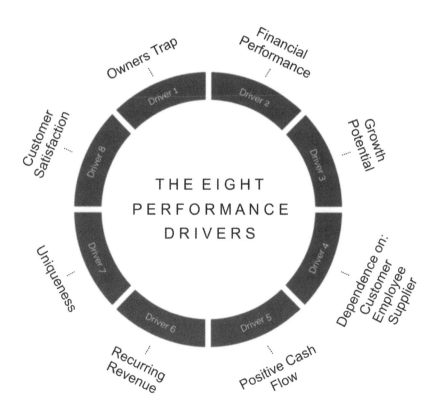

1. The Owner's Trap

2. Uniqueness

3. Customer Satisfaction

4. Growth Potential

5. Customer, Supplier, Employee Dependence

6. Recurring Revenue

7. Positive Cash Flow

8. Financial Performance

I'm going to focus here only on the first two drivers. You can identify the other six drivers from their self-explanatory names. We will be discussing in chapter 9 how we measure them and how they figure into company value.

The Owner's Trap is a measure of whether the business can run independent of the owner. A business in which the owner is doing most of the selling, or all the employees report to that owner, is less valuable than a business set up to perform well in the owner's absence. The dependency can devastate the company's value if something happens to the owner, but it also affects current profitability in various ways. One person has only so much time and attention to spare. One person can get burned out being in a situation where taking time off seems impossible. When employees know they will have to fix problems themselves, they have an incentive to learn to prevent those problems, making the business more efficient.

Uniqueness is a driver that connects to the work we do obliterating obstacles to winning new customers or clients. It requires a business putting in the time and effort to figure out what it should be doing to have the right impact, and whom it should be working with. As Warrillow advised in his book: "Prove that you're serious about specialization by turning down work that falls outside your area of expertise. The more people you say no to, the more referrals you'll get to people who need your product or service."

HABIT 4—USE THE BUDGET TO ENGINEER PROFIT

After the habits take hold of looking at numbers monthly and performing 12-week cash forecasts, it's time to move on to forecasting P&L a year ahead. Since some business owners recoil at the words "budget" and "spreadsheet," I like to call this "creating a flight plan." (Just between us: we do it on a spreadsheet.) We don't really know what's going to happen six months or a year from now, so our forecast probably will be exactly wrong, but it only needs to be in the right zone to be useful. We run through a lot of "what if" scenarios and attach numbers to the most likely outcomes.

	BUDGET	CHANGE	AMOUNT	SCENARIO 1
REVENUE	$1,000,000	1.0%	10,000	$1,010,000
Cost of Sales	628,880	-1.0%	6,289	622,591
Overhead	323,650	-1.0%	3,237	320,414
NET INCOME	47,470		19,525	66,995
% of Revenue	4.7%		41.1%	6.6%

	BUDGET	CHANGE	AMOUNT	SCENARIO 2
REVENUE	$1,000,000	5.0%	50,000	$1,050,000
Cost of Sales	628,880	-1.0%	6,289	622,591
Overhead	323,650	-1.0%	3,237	320,414
NET INCOME	47,470		59,525	106,995
% of Revenue	4.7%		125.4%	10.2%

Some managers mistakenly think having a budget is limiting. If they budget $1 million in sales for the calendar year and reach that point in 10 months, do they think their salespeople will just go home on Halloween and stop selling? Sometimes revenue is over budget, but because you have a budget, you can see in the numbers what you did to become more profitable. Or if you didn't become more profitable, you can see exactly where costs got out of control and where you have been doing better than expected, so you can make timely adjustments to spending and production.

As circumstances change, it's a good idea to reforecast budgets during the year to keep them realistic. If a company acquired more capacity or developed some new efficiency, it should reforecast higher revenue as a result. Some companies reforecast at midyear or at a time that makes sense in their industry because they have passed some seasonal milestone. We are making a flight plan, so we want it to be as accurate as possible. If a storm forces us to change course, we would alter our flight plan and recalculate how long the trip would take with a detour.

A financial flight plan creates options because it is a baseline for evaluating "what if" scenarios whenever they arise. If our profitability is not what we expected, what if we raised all our prices 1 percent? What if we raised only some prices 5 percent instead? We ran a spreadsheet for a client that showed that if the company managed direct costs and overhead each 1 percent better and raised prices 1 percent, those changes would produce a 39 percent boost in profitability. That exercise provides a tremendous incentive to institute changes.

SHOW ME A LINE CHART!

The financial flight plan is not like those 1980s business plans that went on for 300 pages of narrative and ended up sitting in a drawer. It's a spreadsheet the Growth CFO uses to study how current or proposed activities affect P&L. The answers it provides can be displayed visually in charts to aid discussion and decision-making. For example, it often shows that five cost line items make up 80 to 90 percent of total cost, which should prompt a decision to focus cost control on those five items.

Ideas and options for improving profitability can come from anywhere in the company. The Growth CFO's role is to show how those options would play out in the current and future years.

HABIT 5—USE ANALYSIS TO GAIN CLARITY

The first four habits involve using the company's own data, but now it's time to compare the business with its competitors by using an industry benchmark. We use the same database that many banks use to get that "first look loan score" when a business is seeking capital. The database has detailed financial performance numbers for many industries, segmented by geographic location and the revenue levels of the companies.

Whether the company is doing better or worse than competitors on one measure or another is less important than the critical thinking the comparison should stimulate. Asking why the business is falling short of industry averages or doing better than average is a challenge to status quo thinking. No company exactly matches the way it is catego-rized by industry code, but that argument won't go very far when the business is establishing its valuation while seeking a loan or trying to engage in a merger or acquisition. Bankers will use the available data, and you can too, in determining and defending the valuation you seek.

"MY KID IS SPECIAL"

Some CEOs think of their company like it's their child. They push back at being told their kid is not even in the top 40 percentile in their industry segment. But just like when a kid brings home a disappointing report card from school, it's time to ask some questions rather than argue about the grades. "What do we need to do differently to get better results in the future?"

Using macroeconomic assumptions, the CFO can create a multiyear financial flight plan because the timeline of projects and the implications of options do not stop at the end of the budget year. It can be very clarifying to explain how many years a growth objective will take to reach under different scenarios. Sometimes an extended timeline is accept-able. Other times, it's like the wake-up call language on a credit card bill that says, "If

> *Whether the company is doing better or worse than competi-tors on one measure or another is less important than the critical thinking the comparison should stimulate.*

you make no additional charges using this card and each month make the minimum payment, you will pay off the balance shown in this statement in 99 years."

That multiyear forecasting is one of several analyses we do during our first quarter working with clients and repeat at the end of each year in planning for the upcoming year. We also prepare a discounted cash flow valuation to inform what's giving us lift versus drag. We measure the Eight Drivers, do an accounting health check to make sure the controls are strong and the numbers are good, assess opportunities for found money like cost savings and tax credits, and update 80/20 client segment and pricing. That last piece is done with the sales and marketing team as part of the effort to obliterate obstacles to winning new customers and keeping and growing existing customers.

All FIVE Habits discussed in this chapter have self-evident value, but getting them ingrained in a company's management takes a lot of work. Getting started can be intimidating or uncomfortable, like day one of a new exercise regimen. Once habits are ingrained, though, we wonder how we ever got along without them. How could we watch a game without a scoreboard? How could we not try to forecast whether we have enough cash to pay all the bills? Why wouldn't we check whether we are doing better or worse than our competitors? Why wouldn't we line up all the drivers to make sure our long journey ends successfully?

Owners whose businesses can operate independently are better positioned not only to pull income from those businesses but also to get paid a second time when they step back to sell the business or engage in some other type of transition. The next chapter explains how a business owner can Get Paid Twice.

CHAPTER 7

GETTING PAID TWICE

My company had the honor of working with two Vietnam War veterans who used their knowledge of construction and engineering to create a small business building public facilities for the federal government. Nearing retirement, these veterans asked for our help planning to sunset their business. Considering that shutting down would put their employees out of work, we asked, "Why don't you sell the business instead?" It had provided the men a nice income over the years, but if they found a third-party buyer, they would basically Get Paid Twice. There was a catch, they said.

One of the benefits the US government gives military veterans is they receive preference for procurement contracts. A veteran who has a service-connected disability and is a majority owner and top officer of a small business may qualify for a set-aside. They felt the value of their business was so tied into the set-aside program that it would be impossible to find the right buyer. For confidentiality reasons I am fictionalizing the details of this story, but let's say they thought the business was worth $10 million. They figured they would have to find a buyer who was a disabled veteran, knew how to run a construction company, and had access to $10 million, which was more than a long shot.

We worked out a solution in which brokers would find an investor to partner with a qualified veteran. Federal regulations are voluminous and confusing, so our clients, their compliance officer, and their outside counsel all had missed this possibility. It took a lot of legwork for us to find a broker with the right knowledge and contacts to find several dozen prospects to call and put together a short list of potential investment partners. A young dealmaker had built a firm in Philadelphia that specialized in this task. Scrutinizing those prospects and interviewing them with the business owners was the next big job.

Our clients were college-educated men, comfortable in a suit-and-tie business meeting as well as being construction guys. Still, they needed professional guidance to pull off this complicated deal. To properly evaluate bids, they needed to understand how and where prospective buyers would be getting the money, and how this factor would affect the timing and reliability of their payout. The broker might encourage them to accept the biggest bid to get the deal done, but we would help them determine whether that bidder would be able to run the company successfully enough to ensure they eventually got the earn-out they were expecting (this is explained further on page 90). A Small Business Administration cap on loans for this type of purchase would keep them from getting top dollar, but there was a surprise sweetener for the deal: tax credits available for engineering firms that improve the carbon footprint of facilities they work on.

The first bidder found by the broker turned out to be an inexperienced investor with unrealistic expectations. But once they saw how their company could be marketed, the sellers on their own found a better bidder. A young subcontractor in their space, who happened to have a wealthy father-in-law with some money to invest, bought the business.

Seven Succession Options

Many business owners think about succession options too little and too late. It's not hard to guess some reasons why CEOs procrastinate when they think about succession planning. They have more urgent business to deal with, they hope better options are on the horizon, they don't want to predict the future, or they just don't want to think about leaving their baby in the hands of others—especially strangers. Even when they step back and do long-term succession planning, many CEOs consider only a few options of seven that generally are available. This chapter will examine the pros and cons of all seven options.

Financial needs play a major factor in succession planning. For a severely undercapitalized business, agreeing to a merger or acquisition may be necessary for survival. A business owner may have personal financial goals related to retirement, philanthropy, or family needs and desires. These goals can be many years away—another rationalization for putting off planning. But like the parent who starts a college savings fund for a small child, the business owner who works on uniqueness and profitability now will open options later.

Lifestyle considerations also come into play during the planning and the transition. Some business owners cherish free time, and they shouldn't be afraid to tell us they want more of it in the future. I tell them how much I value time with my family, taking care of my two incredibly athletic Belgian Malinois dogs, and entertaining friends around my billiards table, which was exquisitely crafted in the 1880s.

Some CEOs let us know they need a clean break from their business to tend to physical or mental health concerns, family emergencies, or some new priorities in their lives. Others have a hard time imagining stepping away from their work. They may purposely keep their business dependent on them, closing off some succession options.

EARN-OUT PERIOD DEFINED

Sometimes the sale of a business requires the former owner to stay for a transition period, during which the buyer gradually pays an amount based on agreed-upon conditions. This earn-out period, as it is known, is hard to avoid in selling a business that remains dependent on the former owner's expertise or customer relationships. The period averages two and one-half years, during which CEOs are often unhappy with the experience and disappointed with the financial result. They may get trapped into an emotionally draining succession period in which they don't have the same authority that they used to have. Suddenly, they are employees of the company they used to own, which they find frustrating because they remain accountable for getting the business to perform on a certain level to earn the payout they expected.

At Foresight CFO, we always initiate a timely discussion of all seven succession options. The conversation begins with the CFO asking what options the CEO already is aware of and thinking about. We assess each option and its financial and lifestyle impacts. There is no template for this type of conversation, because everyone's circumstances are unique. Beyond personal wishes and needs, the complications include tax strategies, different state laws, and how competitive or niche the business is. The availability of capital fluctuates over time, depending on the economy and what sectors are attracting investors. The one constant principle is that it is never too soon to start planning because doing so informs how you build the business.

Option 1: Next of Kin

Many small business owners imagine at some point that their sons or daughters will want to take over the business, allowing for a smooth transition within the family. But in fact, few businesses pass on that way. Some family businesses are so dependent upon the founder that they cannot succeed after their departure. The sons or daughters may not want the business, because they have different interests. They saw how Mom or Dad—or both—sacrificed and suffered running the business and don't want to live that kind of life. Junior still feels hurt that Dad was too busy to attend his football games and is determined to make it to his son's games.

The one constant principle is that it is never too soon to start planning because doing so informs how you build the business.

When a business owner hands over control to their children, the transition tends to be more gradual than in other succession options. Like a parent letting their kid drive the family car, at the beginning they don't really trust them completely. Some business owners are more ambivalent than others at letting go of control. But even if the businesses can run well independent of the owner, with a next-of-kin ready and willing to take over, this option has potential drawbacks. Children taking over the business usually don't have money to invest in its growth. Any payout to the retiring owner tends to come slowly in installments, rather than in a lump sum. The retiring owner is not freed from worry either, as they'll hear at family dinners about any business problems. Some CEOs find this scenario acceptable because they enjoy watching what happens to their legacy as their children take their company to a higher level.

We worked with a company whose owner's son joined the business and worked his way up from the bottom to be on the executive team. He was well respected and knew the business, so his taking over succeeded. I know of another case in which two business partners did well together, but when the next generation took over, one child stopped contributing to the work and decision-making because of drug use. The ownership arrangement required that the one with the addiction problem still get paid, damaging the partnership.

In considering the next-of-kin option, business owners must ask themselves whether they are choosing the next CEO from a too-limited talent pool.

Option 2: Management Buyout

Company executives may wish to step up and take over. This type of buyout shares some similarities with the previous option. The managers may lack the cash or credit to pay for the company unless they take loans, perhaps risking their home equity as collateral. Sometimes the company takes a loan, and the managers sign off on it with personal guarantees. The seller usually winds up holding a note, with installment payments rather than a lump-sum buyout, but for more money than in an intrafamily purchase. If the business has a lot of tangible assets, such as factory equipment or a fleet of trucks, management may need less money than in a company relying on intangible assets, such as highly paid software developers.

A management team can raise only so much money to buy the business, but they may have strong potential to continue the owner's legacy and further build the company's value. If the CEO has been hiring wisely and delegating responsibility, the business will be in good hands, allowing the owner to exit quickly and move on to enjoying retirement or other opportunities. Sometimes, the death or impairment of a CEO prompts a rushed management buyout, but ideally any type of buyout follows at least two or three years of preparation. The owners should work themselves out of having areas of business dependent on them. They need time to hire people to fill key roles and make sure the initial hires work out. Some companies have an entrepreneurial culture, and their management teams are up to being owners. The opposite is true at other companies.

A variation of management buyout often occurs at firms of doctors, lawyers, or other professionals. New partners buy in and take over patients or clients who might otherwise be lost to competing firms.

Option 3: Employee Stock Ownership Plan

An employee stock ownership plan (ESOP) is a mechanism that allows the company to set up a trust on behalf of the employees to essentially buy the business. To be clear, the employees are not putting up money or becoming owners as individuals. The company is funding the trust, usually with a bank loan or a note held by the seller. The CEO and management team report to the ESOP governing body. When that committee hires effectively and the company makes money, the employees will share in the profits.

As of 2021, the National Center for Employee Ownership estimated there were about 6,600 ESOPs covering more than 14 million participants, and about two-thirds of the ESOPs were used to buy shares of a departing owner of a profitable, closely held company.[8] The number of such plans decreased in recent years, although the total number of participants rose. I believe this option has enough benefits that it would be more common if it were better understood. An ESOP can be a cost-effective way for an owner to get cash out of a company to retire or move on while giving loyal employees continuity that might be lost in a takeover by a competitor.

ESOPs take time and effort to put together, and they won't work for all situations. The company must document its financial strength and growth outlook. Months of work go into the underwriting process when a bank examines the company's financial reports to determine how big a loan it can handle. The company must have enough revenue or sales to justify the ongoing administrative costs. In my experience, an annual top line of $10 million is the threshold for recouping costs. Like a 401(k) plan, the ESOP comes with compliance requirements. If the business owner sells only a portion of the company shares, in what's called a partial liquidity event, that seller remains on the hook for some of the administrative costs. The benefit of a partial liquidity event for the seller is retaining some ownership but backing out enough cash to enjoy life or diversify into other assets rather than having it all tied up in one business.

---

8   "Employee Ownership by the Numbers," National Center for Employee Ownership, March 2021, https://www.nceo.org/articles/employee-ownership-by-the-numbers.

Option 4: Third-Party Buyer

The merger and acquisition option is by far the most common way for a business owner to get paid on the way out the door. Sometimes an offer comes uninvited. Businesses that reach a certain level of revenue and visibility start getting cold calls from private equity firms or representatives of other types of investors. Companies that would welcome such attention should plan on maintaining the financial data to know and show what they are worth. CEOs should be careful about sharing proprietary data with unknown callers, who may just be fishing for competitive insights. Instead of just hoping the right suitor comes along at the right time, business owners should be proactive. They should make a short list of ideal third-party buyers, study them, talk to them, and intentionally build the business to be attractive to those companies or investors. For our clients, the Growth CFOs conduct initial talks to validate potential buyers.

When the business owner has built something that has strategic value to another company, the payoff can be amazing. People around the world were shocked in 2014 when Facebook agreed to pay $19 billion in cash and stock for an unprofitable five-year-old company. By the time the sale closed, Facebook paid more than $21 billion for WhatsApp because Facebook's stock value rose after Wall Street digested the news of its purchase of a messaging app that had 500 million users and was growing every day. But your business doesn't have to be a household name to be a strategic M&A (merger and acquisition) target.

Suppose you have 50 clients, and another company has 50,000 clients that match the description of your ideal prospect. The other company is better positioned than you are to steer your company toward astronomical growth by leveraging its existing relationships.

After acquiring your company, it can offer your product or service to those 50,000 clients. If only 1 percent take up the offer, your business will grow tenfold, or by 1,000 percent. If your net revenue per client has averaged $50,000, that $2.5 million business will become a $25 million brand in the larger company's portfolio. Or maybe the synergy will cause the revenue to grow even greater.

Besides the strategic buyers and private equity firms, individuals sometimes buy a company simply because they want to own one. Perhaps they ran a similar company or got passed over to be CEO at another company and need a new challenge. Whatever their motivation, it is probably less compelling to the target company than a strategic buyer's quest for synergy. The best-case scenario for the seller is to attract multiple strategic buyers at the same time to compare a variety of offers.

It's no secret that some M&As don't go well for everyone involved. Companies overpay or get underpaid because they miscalculate valuation. Your competitor, supplier, or some CEO wannabe who doesn't know enough about your business could buy it based on a flawed or unrealistic strategy and run it into the ground. Your longtime, loyal employees could be cast out as expendable, and your clients and customers could be abandoned. Due diligence and expert advisors can help avoid missteps, but investment bankers have explained to me that roughly three-quarters of M&A proposals still fall through once due diligence starts. Business owners also must ask themselves the right questions: What is their objective? Have they done the work to determine and maximize the value of their business? How much money do they need to live the kind of life they want?

Other times a sale goes better than hoped for. Somebody unexpected shows up with a use for your product or service you never thought of. We have had clients who thought there was no way to sell their business, but we helped them find the right investment banker or broker to take them to market, and we were by their side to get the deal done.

Option 5: Retiring Partway

Some business owners don't want to run day-to-day operations anymore but are not ready to retire fully. The solution for them is hiring a general manager, so they are free to work on whatever they want. This option can have a very positive lifestyle impact, but the financial ramifications depend on the profitability of the business. A good general manager might bring leadership continuity, energy, and new ideas to the business, increasing its value.

This option allows an owner to get paid gradually, avoiding the tax consequences of a big payout. If the owner subsequently passes away, and the general manager is ready to step up as CEO, the estate avoids a succession crisis. The big pitfall is that it is easy to hire, or promote from within, the wrong person. Some business owners go through two or three general managers before they find someone with the right skills and personality. The owner's control issues or conflicts among the management team can interfere with a smooth transition. Business owners interested in this option should start early to give it time to work and give themselves time to adjust and let go. In a hybrid of options 3 and 5, an owner can sell a portion of company shares to an ESOP, maintain majority control, and have a general manager run the business.

Option 6: Go Public

Preparing an initial public offering (IPO) is an expensive, time-consuming prospect, but it promises great financial benefits for some companies. I'll leave giving advice about how and whether to do an IPO to the specialists a company would have to hire for that purpose. A business owner embarking on an IPO can hire lawyers and accountants to do the legwork but also should expect personally to take on a new set of responsibilities. Running a public company requires meeting with analysts and investors, doing road shows, and being the public face of your business.

Compliance and reporting requirements force a business that goes public to adopt new policies and procedures. The roles of officers are so different that a company might have to change out its management team to get the necessary skills and experience. A lot of people who work well in a nonpublic environment just would not be happy or effective managing a public company. As with the other options, CEOs must examine their personal needs and objectives carefully before proceeding.

If a company has products or services that have broadly captured the public's imagination, an IPO can fuel more growth than the other options. A variation that has become more popular lately is the special purpose acquisition company (SPAC). Being acquired by a SPAC allows your company to operate within a shell company that's already public.

Option 7: Sunset the Business

The easiest but least rewarding option is to close the business. If you include all the sole proprietorships and small partnerships in the universe of small businesses, this is the dominant way owners close up shop. They have created a business dependent on them, and nobody else wants it, so it is not transferable.

In the best-case scenario, the owners get some money by liquidating assets, and they arrange for their clients, customers, or employees to land elsewhere. But this option basically is the default when owners feel they have no other choices. An example I have seen of owners being satisfied with this option is when children inherit a mom-and-pop business they want no part of. Liquidation provides the children both closure and freedom.

> *In the best-case scenario, the owners get some money by liquidating assets, and they arrange for their clients, customers, or employees to land elsewhere.*

A business owner who has put off planning for succession or has thought about only a few of the seven options we covered in this chapter may be missing out greatly on financial and lifestyle benefits. Maybe retirement is years down the road, but the financial management, tax strategy, and planning work done now opens options. Developing the Habits of Profitability puts in place the financial resources for a lucrative exit. The next chapter explains how my company guides the CEO on that journey.

CHAPTER 8

90-DAY SPRINTS

O
ur Australian branch brought in a client with the audacious goal of quintupling its business. The idea that the company could turbocharge its growth seemed fitting since it manufactures a component popular with car owners who want to maximize engine performance. We provided the client a couple of Growth CFOs who happen to love cars, but who also understand how to generate the numbers banks would require to provide access to capital on favorable terms. Our initial evaluation found this company was well managed using tools provided by an Entrepreneurial Operating System (EOS) consultant to keep track of its international business. We found that to fuel the desired growth it would have to develop global banking relationships it lacked and make a business case to lenders about its potential.

This client was fun to work with but had a complicated multichannel business because it sold direct to consumers around the world, to automakers, and to specialty shops. It also had brand reputation-building tie-ins with auto racing teams. Offices in the US and UK generated revenue that was repatriated to the home office in Australia, where the CFO oversaw the accounting. The strategic work we were doing did not conflict with the excellent controller-type function the existing CFO was performing, and she was happy to have us step in just as she was going on maternity leave. Another quite different life-changing event facing the company was Brexit. The European operation was run out of the UK, so there was a lot of bureaucracy and paperwork to deal with before it could expand in Europe.

Businesses are complicated, people are complicated, and political cataclysms like Brexit are really complicated, but our job was to provide clarity and confidence to the CEO. We needed to give him something simple and easy to understand: a rolling 24-month cash forecast would make clear how much money was available for initiatives. As an early step, we trained the general managers in the US and UK to deliver some numbers monthly in a standard format resembling a 90-second elevator pitch: "This year I am expecting to finish (this many dollars or pounds sterling) ahead of last year in revenue." Key expenses would be summed up with similar brevity in a way that was consistent month after month.

"We never really looked at the business like this," one of the top executives said. The general managers felt confident going into monthly financial review meetings because they knew what data they were supposed to be providing and how they were expected to say it. The exchange of information was not for bragging rights. It was intended to help make decisions necessary for growth of the business. The home office would find out how much cash might be arriving from the regions to fund its capital expenditures. And once those needs were met, more money could be left in the regions to fuel their growth. The business needed that global coordination to run on all cylinders.

Everything I just described was accomplished in a 90-day sprint that was focused on getting the company started on the flight plan to fulfilling its primary goal. It's easy to write a five-year plan at a very high level that points toward a goal. But we have found that setting out a clear path each quarter, to be updated before the next quarter, is where the magic happens.

Identifying One Compelling Outcome

For Foresight CFO to provide clients a multiyear financial flight plan, we really need to get to know them first. As in any good relationship, we begin with a discovery discussion. In that initial conversation, we discuss the Five Obstacles to Growth and how they are affecting the company, and we identify one compelling outcome the CEO wants. From there, we are ready to make a service proposal for a three-person TrueTEAM to implement in a 90-day sprint. Often, we have been called in because a company is stalled, but we are not there to jump-start it with some prepackaged recommendations for changes. We need to investigate, analyze, think, and plan what is appropriate for the specific company and industry.

Within the first few weeks, we roll up our sleeves and do a complete financial health check, the forensic accounting equivalent of an MRI full-body scan. Sometimes, we find pleasant surprises, like easy cost savings or a big tax credit the client's accountant overlooked. We are establishing ourselves as a trusted navigator for the CEO's full journey to succession, so creating instant ROI that pays for years of our services goes a long way. It is not unusual to identify a quarter-million dollars of found money, which is a great *wow* factor to get a CEO's enthusiastic attention and support for moving forward. Poor accounting practices, such as equipment not being depreciated or errors in accrual, can cause a company's books to overstate expenses and provide a distorted picture of profitability. Other times, the results of the financial health check are disappointing, like when a business has been burning through too much cash or making decisions based on bad numbers. Poor accounting practices can understate expenses and overstate revenue.

EASY COST SAVINGS

When small, private companies negotiate with vendors, they rarely get as good a price as the big guys. But there are experts who know ways to overcome this disadvantage, such as pooling the purchasing power of a lot of small companies. We figure out which cost-saving specialists our clients should use in buying computers, health insurance, telecommunication services, and so on. Our accounting health check also may save money by turning up billing errors or duplicated payments. The impact can be substantial if, for example, a flawed billing code was systematically preventing customers from being charged for some product or service for a long period of time.

We create two years of financial reports and five years of financial forecasts in a database. It looks like a spreadsheet, which is enough to make a lot of CEOs recoil, until they see what it can do for them. We can use it to provide insights in our accompanying narrative into how different scenarios will affect the valuation of the business over time. We can change one variable in the database and see how it affects all the others. The idea is to find the best way to get from where the company is to where it wants to be, Obliterating Obstacles to Growth one step at a time. The timelines for reaching goals vary by company.

Moving Confidently into Action

Our initial assessment has quite an impact on our clients when we present a chief-level briefing on what we have found in the first few weeks. We also give the CEO a written report with an executive summary running about five pages that includes supporting details, such as a proposed action plan that can begin immediately during the first 90-day sprint. That tight time frame has proven effective for focusing on one outcome that is a top priority for them.

It is not unusual to identify a quarter-million dollars of found money, which is a great wow factor to get a CEO's enthusiastic attention and support for moving forward.

We can move quickly from our analytical work to an action plan. We already have learned what the CEO wants—for example, to grow revenue from $15 million to $50 million. We already have made the first iteration of a multiyear flight plan to that goal, giving the CEO a realistic sense of how many years it would take. When CEOs receive our assessment, some of them find out they were overly optimistic about what they want to do, and they need to get realistic. Some find out that what they want to do is possible, but they need to overcome obstacles by increasing capacity or funding in ways they didn't realize. They may need to put more money into sales, marketing, or delivery. All those budget items are in the flight plan, and we can adjust them to show

how different scenarios are likely to play out. We compare profitability to other companies in the same industry and use benchmarks as a further guide to decision-making.

Running through "what if" scenarios and considering the pros and cons is time well spent when there are numbers showing what is realistic. It is not a blue-sky exercise. Discussion of investing in this or that is based on actual cash or projected revenue. Some CEOs discover they need to trim their expectations, particularly in mature industries. There are companies in fields ranging from biotechnology to gaming that are capable of tremendous growth if they make the right moves. But they can't take their year-over-year growth for granted, because products have a life cycle, patents expire, and competition can be fierce, among other variables.

In our flight plan, valuation of a company is based on forward forecast cash flow. Of course, we are making some key assumptions, which we spell out. Some options we recommend assume that a company can find new clients or create new products, which is a risky proposition. We have ways to display these options graphically in our recommendations to make clear which ones are safer or riskier.

Oh, the Possibilities!

A common factor that stalls business growth is being trapped in a race to the bottom on pricing. A company is chasing any and all customers by offering the lowest prices in its market. We can run "what if" scenarios on raising prices or focusing on providing greater value to a higher-end niche market. It is fun to imagine being able to raise prices 15, 20, or 30 percent, but figuring out the impact is another matter. Business owners know intuitively that the higher end of the market has more money, and the bottom end has a lot more customers. What they need to see in black and white numbers is how much profit they are making with the current customer base and what exactly they could change to attract enough customers who don't commoditize their goods or services.

The COVID-19 pandemic was a case study in businesses having to respond to market shifts because of supply disruptions and the economic impact being so uneven across the population. Furniture makers, for example, encountered more demand than they could supply for the higher-end home goods being bought up by the people fortunate enough to be able to work from home. One of our clients sells furniture in a wealthy suburb where the pandemic prompted people who normally spend money on travel, entertainment, and dining out to shift that spending to buying and furnishing bigger homes.

We had another client, a first-time business owner, who was ready to shut down his company after a disastrous 2020. COVID-19 directly affected demand for his services, and he couldn't foresee recovering without investing substantially in modifications. The path forward felt too daunting because of the psychological toll of living through the pandemic and watching his business shrivel. The ability to run "what if" scenarios with the data in his financial flight plan provided the reassurance he needed to press on and gradually turn the corner from his business losses.

When we talk about changes that will have impact, they don't necessarily involve major investments or shifts in market strategy. Sometimes the numbers point to being able to tweak prices or cost management practices just a little bit. A company can beta test whether raising prices 1 percent or making a small quality improvement would be worthwhile. If it seems promising, the financial flight plan will show the long-term impact of doing it across the product line. Sometimes a company doesn't realize that its bottom line has been depressed by falling into a practice that is out of line with the industry. Maybe it is not managing its inventory well and needs to sell off goods that are taking up valuable space for months longer than normal. We found that one client was unusually prompt at paying bills within 30 days in an industry where 90 days was common. We could show the client how much more cash it would have by changing that pattern and what it could do with that cash.

Observing and Questioning

The work involved in the first 90-day sprint requires a lot more than number crunching. We were working remotely and using technology to hold meetings and compile data long before it became commonplace in 2020, so it takes us no time to join the team. But a site visit can be eye opening. When we see inventory piled up, gathering dust, we know inventory turnover time is one of the statistics we'll be focusing on. When a company can't answer some basic questions about how it makes and spends money, we know that we'll be training managers in budget preparation. When frontline workers are eager to tell us what their workplace is missing, we know we'll be analyzing the potential impact of purchasing new equipment, supplies, or software. We build rapport and trust with the client's people by asking open-ended questions, and not "leading the witness." They tell us about best practices or opportunities for improvement they are taking up or missing out on in their industry, which they understand better than us.

An important tool in our observation and analysis is measuring the Eight Drivers, which we introduced in chapter 6 when we were discussing the third of the FIVE Habits of Profitability: Create Succession Options to Get Paid Twice. It's important to know which of the drivers have the most impact on business performance, so we ask about that, and how they may have changed over time. Has the business become more or less dependent on one owner, supplier, or customer? Is the product still unique? Is recurring revenue still recurring?

A best practice for us when possible is to go back on site quarterly and repeat the flight plan evaluation annually. Business owners may fail to notice slowly changing conditions that affect profitability, like their trucks going from 80 percent full to 70 percent full. They may be paying too much rent because their head count dropped, and the remaining employees spread out in the same space. As we update the flight plan, we see which numbers are changing, which are not, and how the interplay of those numbers is affecting the bottom line.

One Top Priority

As we ask questions, compile the answers, and upload data into our flight plan, we do not want to overload ourselves and our client by trying to use it all. Our analysis should result in one top priority, and possibly a second or third thing that must be addressed as action items. In our discovery conversation before we begin the initial evaluation, we identify one compelling outcome the business owner personally would like to achieve, such as a comfortable retirement. The top priority for the company is a related, but less personal, business objective.

The best way to determine a top priority is to follow the numbers. We use a mix of our own proprietary evaluation tools and ones we subscribe to because of their proven reliability. The data will show whether a company's cash flow is hitting industry benchmarks, whether it is rising or falling steadily, varies by season, or is fluctuating wildly. The numbers will show if the company's performance falters whenever the CEO goes on vacation. We will see whether current products and prices have shrinking profit margins, or if certain customer segments are not worth the expense of keeping. Looking at the various measurements, one or more will stand out as having the most impact.

Practicing what we preach, Foresight CFO developed its own platform that we lovingly call Impact. It combines project management with keeping track of team members' performance, starting with their onboarding, and tracing their continuous training and their assignments to projects, tasks, and clients. The same platform shows how we are addressing the clients' priorities and what work we have set aside for later. Information that might otherwise be scattered into hundreds or thousands of emails is in one place where any authorized team member can retrieve it. We compile key performance indicators by tracking data such as completed or overdue tasks. These KPIs help us prioritize our work.

Reaching Next-Level Clarity

Big public companies usually track their financial objectives and performance in an organized and effective way, but smaller private companies often fail to do so. They can't answer some basic questions we ask in our initial assessment about the money they are spending or what their customers are doing. We don't expect any of our clients to have all the data we would like to put into our flight plan, but the more we can fill in, using hypothetical scenarios or educated guesses if necessary, the better it works. Finding out that a client can't provide certain data doesn't stop us from proceeding. It informs us about steps needed to give that client clarity. We are finding out together with the clients that they have blind spots.

Frequently, our new clients don't have enough visibility into their finances and operations because they have not learned the FIVE Habits of Profitability that we discussed in chapter 6.

A stubborn problem persists at all kinds of businesses despite abundant advice to avoid it: managers working on achieving their goals in isolation from each other. A multitude of research proves that the most successful companies identify the right goals with the full participation of the management team. Clearly, that's easier said than done. A CEO can't just order it to happen immediately because managers must develop skills and habits like the elevator-pitch summary of revenue and expenses that branch managers of the Australian company learned to deliver.

Obtaining clarity about where a business stands on the road to its desired outcome requires measuring performance in many ways. Some employees may need to track their activities hourly or weekly. Top managers should be reporting their financial results monthly. This tracking or reporting enables and supports the 90-day sprints even when it is not directly relevant to the one or few current top priorities.

Showing Impact Quarterly

As the 90 days end, we report the outcome to the CEO and make recommendations for the next sprint, using all the performance measures we have available. This chief-level discussion makes clear, using visuals, what was accomplished, or not, and why. The talking points may be challenging, but they are full of analysis and insight. We set priorities and action items for the next sprint. This is not just another meeting like the weekly huddles we have been having with managers to follow up on the sprint's objectives. This quarterly session can be really rewarding for both the CEO and the Growth CFO. It's like when a jetliner flight descends through the clouds and a panoramic view of the destination appears. It is a chance to slow down and enjoy the clear view of where the business is going.

Obtaining clarity about where a business stands on the road to its desired outcome requires measuring performance in many ways.

Clients tell us they can feel the teamwork that results from walls coming down and managers being better aligned as a result of the sprint. The quarterly review may reveal some issues or constraints, but seeing them clearly and having a plan to address them leave the CEO feeling confident.

Keeping Audacious Goals Realistic

Many CEOs feel let down by the tendency of their people to tell them what they want to hear. They welcome realistic assessments based on solid numbers. We were able to tell our Australian client's CEO that his audacious growth goal was achievable. Our assessment was based on combining the insights we got from his various departments— manufacturing, operations, sales, and support services. We didn't have any special expertise about the market for his product. But from our observations and analysis, we would chart a course for the multiyear goal and recognize what to commit to accomplish in the first 90 days.

When the client's desired outcome appears unrealistic, invariably the cause involves what we discussed in chapter 6 as the FIVE Habits of Profitability. Typically, the business has fallen short in the third habit, developing the Eight Drivers of business value. Financial performance and growth potential are below par; it is too dependent on the owner or certain suppliers, customers, or employees; or it doesn't have the necessary positive cash flow, recurring revenue, uniqueness, or customer satisfaction.

The priority of the first 90-day sprint might be to improve one of these drivers, for example by assessing whether it can take a unique new product to market. At the same time, we're building the Habits of Profitability. We are making sure the business has monthly financial reports with good numbers. We are making a 12-week cash forecast. That work sets a Foresight Growth CFO apart from a consultant who would focus only on the goal—marketing that new product. Our approach is more realistic because it gives the CEO a clear view of the future consequences of the current plan. What must be done to ensure the business will have the capacity to meet demand for the new product if it succeeds? Will it need a line of credit? Does it have the financial records needed to secure that credit? We work with managers to develop these capabilities.

Following the Cash

At first, the best read we can get on some clients' cash flow comes from their current bank balance. We gradually build from that narrow view by seeing week by week what cash comes in, customer by customer, and what goes out, vendor by vendor. We are measuring the cash conversion cycle, which tells a company how long, before or after it spends money on inventory, production, sales, or whatever, it will take in money from its operations. Some companies will never have a positive cash flow in which the money comes in before it must be spent. But measuring how long it takes them to bill and get paid tells them how much cash they need.

Developing a 12-week cash forecast is an important early step on the road to financial clarity. Every business should do it, regardless of whether you hire Foresight CFO. When we are on our first 90-day sprint with a client, the cash forecast is a tool we use to provide financial rigor to whatever analysis or actions are getting underway. Let's say the company is considering launching a new product, which a consultant says will provide an excellent return on investment. The consultant may be a subject-matter expert who can advise what it takes to produce, deliver, and market that product but be blind to the issue of whether the company will have enough money at the right time to do so successfully. We are helping clients get information they need about how to pursue their priority, while we also assess how reasonable their goals are given their financial reality. Sometimes we have to say, "You don't have the money to do that," but we're there to help them develop a Plan B.

Looking at All the Numbers

Available cash is just one number among many that affect business plans during the 90-day sprints. Unrealistic numbers get thrown about all too often in executive suites. One memorable case went something like this at a company that served a small niche and really wanted to grow: The company's marketing list vendor recommended a mailing targeted at 250,000 people, but management was not satisfied with the forecast results. They wanted twice as much revenue. "This is scalable, right? Let's mail 500,000 people, and then we can hit our revenue target," an enthusiastic manager said. That's when the finance person interjected, "How do you know there are 500,000 names available?" There weren't half a million realistic prospects that could be identified in the whole country, given the target demographics and specialized interests involved. Due diligence must be applied to every planned action.

Our discussion of the FIVE Habits of Profitability started off with two habits involving keeping an eye on numbers: Achieve Positive Cash Flow and Drive Impact with the Financial Scoreboard. In our proprietary project management system, KPIs provide both the measurable outcome of the 90-day sprint and early warning if something's amiss. It's like when a pilot sees a landmark that doesn't match the flight plan. Did you go off course, or did you map out the journey wrong? Are you going to keep going without taking time to figure out where you're at?

A weekly or even daily look at a KPI dashboard ensures a company has not gotten off course in its overall financial flight plan. The KPIs focus on a small section of the plan. Individual managers can look at the KPIs relevant to their realms and say, "Hey, I'm doing better than expected," which is great for morale. If they are doing worse than expected, at least they know, so they can quickly adjust. Some CEOs needlessly worry their people will slack off if the numbers show they are exceeding goals. There's no time for that to happen if the CEO is reviewing results quarterly with an eye toward determining priorities for the next 90-day sprint.

Executing the Plan

We give CEOs an executive summary of the results of the sprint, supported by some 30 pages of analysis and details, to prepare for a conversation about what's been accomplished and what comes next. Every company has its customized action plan, but they all have one underlying thing in common: incremental development of those FIVE Habits of Profitability. If the company has no detailed 12-week

cash forecast, the first sprint may start with the accounting department sending the CEO a weekly report on cash in the bank, and it
may end with our being able to provide a four-week cash forecast.
Then, we can extend that incrementally to eight weeks and 12 weeks
in the next sprint.

Quality financial management systems take time to implement,
but we proceed under the maxim that perfection is the enemy of
the good. We do not delay starting to shape good habits even if the
initial efforts are far from ideal. The first time we meet with some
management teams to discuss their profit and loss statement can be
eye opening if they have never done this before. A lot of work goes
into producing an accurate report and explaining why we are doing
it, because reviewing it can be emotionally challenging for the CEO
and other managers.

CEOs have offered various reasons why they are reluctant to
share financial data with managers. When the numbers are good,
they think managers will demand more money for themselves or their
departments. They think bad numbers will lower morale or scare away
good managers. When they are discussing priorities with a Foresight
CFO, however, they soon realize the role accurate numbers play: we
are asking a lot of questions, and the answers are in those numbers.

What would you like to know about your business that you
don't know? You want to know how much of your product you are
selling through which stores? You want to know which stores sell
the most and which sell the least? What if your retail sales manager,
Rita, could answer those questions each month and clearly explain
how and why the numbers had changed? What if Rita could forecast
future sales and tell you each month which stores' sales were over or
under the forecast? What if she could explain why this happened in
a way all the other managers understood and offer suggested changes

in strategy? Most CEOs would be relieved to have managers taking ownership that way.

CEOs who get their management teams into the habit of clearly explaining performance results during weekly or monthly meetings see the resulting calibration and teamwork. If sales are forecast to rise or fall, inventory and capacity of production and delivery must be adjusted. As one manager is speaking, the gears in the others' heads are moving. "Uh oh, I'm going to have to fill those vacancies fast" or "Maybe I should hold off signing that new warehouse lease." This coordination is routine in well-run large organizations. But smaller, privately held companies often fail to align their divisions. Short-staffed, hands-on managers may feel they don't have time to attend meetings. They may feel they know everything that's happening at their small company. But we see attitudes change when the financial scoreboard Habit 2 takes hold. After three months they can't make decisions without seeing numbers.

Checking the Forecast

By the second 90-day sprint, we want to introduce Habit 3: use the budget to engineer profit. Now that we have clarity into the company's profit and loss, we can build a budget forecast. Companies arrive at this point from a lot of different places. Some companies have budget forecasts, but they are sitting on a shelf, leaving no easy way to compare current results to what was forecast. Some managers fear the account-ability that would result from such comparisons. At other companies, the CEO sees budget forecasting as a distraction from "real work." That attitude is hard to overcome. Some people are convinced that budgeting is an administrative burden because they worked at companies where it was performed in a time-wasting, bureaucratic way.

In chapters 3, 4, and 5, we discussed the need to forecast expenses and the risks of not budgeting. In chapter 6 we explained how we overcome the reluctance of some CEOs and managers to make a budget. They think that nobody can predict the future, and that it somehow puts a ceiling on initiatives. We talk over these fears and explain how budgets need to be only approximately right to be helpful. Wasting time chasing down variances in small numbers doesn't make sense, given our understanding of the 80/20 principle, which holds that roughly 20 percent of customers or 20 percent of marketing efforts generate 80 percent of revenue.

We take the pressure off managers by helping them learn the process and assuring them their forecasts don't have to be perfect. We will work with them side by side, but they key in the numbers because they are the ones accountable. If the CFO puts together the numbers, the managers do not have ownership of their budgets. Meanwhile, we are having weekly calls with the CEO reviewing progress. While overall objectives don't usually change, priorities may be adjusted based on details we are uncovering. The financial flight plan is never stamped "Final Version" and sent off to be laminated.

STAYING CONSISTENT

Some CEOs are mile-a-minute thinkers. If they want to change their company's priorities dozens of times a day, we can't work with them. Our process of quarterly planning and reviews relies on maintaining consistent objectives. When priorities change based on intentional planning, managers and staff can adjust, but no business can shift course as fast as the human mind can dream up new ideas.

Getting Habits Ingrained

Our efforts to instill the FIVE Habits of Profitability pay off through-out the year in better decision-making, but especially so in October when a company is planning for the upcoming year. It's a smart time to focus on Habit 5: Use Analysis to Gain Clarity. These financial figures enable a company to measure its success in one dimension, but there is a second dimension we consider—peace of mind. CEOs should be confident of where they are going and that their team members are on board. Looking ahead at a full year also encourages Habit 3's longer-term focus on developing the drivers to Get Paid Twice.

Let's look at what happened to a couple of the entrepreneurs we introduced earlier in the book. Chapter 1 introduced you to the cofounders of Envision EMI, who enjoyed both financial success and peace of mind. Their annual salaries increased tenfold, and they were able to step away from the office and enjoy life even before they sold the business for enough money to give their families multigenerational wealth. At the beginning of chapter 5, we discussed a company poised for growth because it specialized in technology that was becoming more popular and essential. But peace of mind was an issue for the CEO of Tsawesome Corp., as we called it. Getting a handle on his ebbing cash flow and establishing an unassailable valuation allowed him to get the strategic buyout he wanted at a higher price than he expected. In the next chapter, you will meet doctors who gained both financial rewards and peace of mind by embracing the Habits of Profitability. Their income more than doubled as they made more productive use of resources, and one doctor who earned less than his partner finally understood why.

Watching business leaders grow more sophisticated in over-coming the Five Obstacles to Growth by confidently applying the

FIVE Habits of Profitability and celebrating with them as they enjoy successes has created a fulfilling career for an increasing number of Foresight Growth CFOs. If you have read this far, you probably want to know if the Foresight CFO way is right for your company. The next chapter explains what help is available for a CEO who really wants to have a growth company but is stuck in some of the ways we have discussed.

CHAPTER 9
FILL THE VOID

Y ou would think the owners of any business partnership would meet regularly to discuss their financial results and how to distribute or reinvest profits. In the real world, that discussion doesn't always happen, as we saw when we got to know two doctors who owned a medical specialty clinic in the Midwest. One of the doctors hired us initially to look into his concern that he was getting less money than he expected. That concern raised a red flag that fraud might be occurring, but the true problem was in the compensation structure of the medical practice. The way Americans pay for healthcare is notoriously complicated, and doctors generally don't have the time or interest to master and oversee all the details of billing codes and insurance payments. The two doctors had a general written agreement about how they would get paid, but it had not kept up with changes over the years and left a lot of room for judgment calls by the office manager.

As we investigated the financial structure of the medical practice, it became clear that there was no communication between the doctors about business issues. One doctor or the other might tell the office manager about a staffing or equipment need, and the doctors no doubt collaborated on patient care, but they never sat down to review their finances together. It's not unusual for professionals to be consumed with their day-to-day practice and stay within their areas of expertise and confidence. In fact, many law firm partners and all kinds of smart business owners avoid financial analysis and planning because that work is outside their comfort zones.

When a Foresight CFO visited to make an initial evaluation, what ensued was not a meeting with the two doctors and the office manager, but something more like shuttle diplomacy. The CFO's first step was to piece together how the business worked, including how fixed and variable costs were allocated. If one doctor spends a day doing surgery highly compensated by insurance and the other spends the day providing treatments that produce low billing, how are the costs of shared services such as staff and medical supplies allocated? We had to understand those basics before we could propose changes that would address the issue of the one doctor making less money than the other.

In the end, both doctors agreed to hire Foresight CFO to make their practice more profitable. They gained clarity on how their business worked, agreed to make the expense allocation fairer, and realized they could bring in another doctor or two to make more cost-effective use of their facilities and equipment. They were able to make a difficult but necessary decision on whether to invest in the growth of a small side practice, which they decided to sell instead. We also arranged for three companies to review their billing, with the doctors remaining anonymous. That exercise showed they could collect 32 percent more revenue for the same work by coding procedures differently. Getting there involved changing billing vendors and their staff being trained on new software.

A medical practice is an unusual business in some ways, even beyond the complexity of its billing. Two practitioners could bring in different amounts of revenue doing almost the same work if one is more energetic or knows newer procedures, or if one is constrained by the policies of the patients' insurers. But the underlying issues we addressed are quite common across many industries: lack of clarity about the business, disagreement about cost allocations, and over-looked inefficiencies.

The Foresight CFO walked into a difficult interpersonal situation after being hired by one of the two doctors but did not play favorites. Taking a neutral position, asking questions, listening, trying to be authentic, the CFO developed trust and won over the second doctor as a client too. People can sniff out hidden agendas, and we never have one. The work we have done with capacity utilization in other kinds of businesses allowed us to see something the doctors could not see: their household income would go up markedly if a third or fourth doctor was brought in to use idle equipment and office space. Small businesses keep people like the office manager of the medical practice busy processing bills and making payments, and they don't have time to analyze financial performance. We do, and I'll explain in this chapter how clients engage with us.

People can sniff out hidden agendas, and we never have one.

Flight Plans and Habits

Throughout this book we have been comparing the Growth CFO to a navigator who sits with the pilot on the flight deck throughout a well-planned journey. Are you thinking this metaphor is nonstop and has landed at its final destination? No, it has continuing service, taking us through a brief recap of the FIVE Habits of Profitability. Developing these habits with managers is fundamental to the work we do with CEOs to overcome the Five Obstacles to Growth.

- **Habit 1—Achieve Positive Cash Flow.** For any business, cash is like fuel in the tank. Commercial airlines manage their fuel so there is enough, but not so much that excessive weight hurts fuel economy. Planes are not allowed to take off with broken fuel gauges. But too many small, private businesses operate without the equivalent 12-week cash forecasts, much less the 12-month rolling forecasts they need for the long haul.

- **Habit 2—Drive Impact with the Financial Scoreboard.** The financial reports and KPIs that a Growth CFO develops and reviews regularly with the CEO are like the cockpit dashboard instruments that tell a pilot where the plane is in comparison with its flight plan.

- **Habit 3—Develop the Eight Drivers to Get Paid Twice.** A strong team and great instruments can't make up for a pilot not being familiar with the route or having a clear view of the destination. A pilot—or a CEO—must be motivated to perform at a high level. You wouldn't want to get into a plane with a pilot who had a "Why does it matter?" attitude or didn't have a clear sense of the drivers that maintain the aircraft's speed and altitude.

- **Habit 4—Use the Budget to Engineer Profit.** A flight plan must cover not only the beginning of a journey but all planned takeoffs and landings. There must be enough fuel, or the possibility of refueling, to reach the next destination if unexpected delays or diversions happen. Budgeting for failure sounds scary, so we prefer to call it resourcing risk. A company's financial flight plan forecasts how it will weather ups and downs, and not only in its current year, which is like the first leg of a multicity flight.

- **Habit 5—Use Analysis to Gain Clarity.** Studying the competitive landscape is like the pilot being familiar with the topography and layout of runways at the destination. Not knowing the company's valuation is like not knowing how long a runway the plane needs if it must make an emergency landing.

Investing in Growth

A CEO who really wants to have a growth company and is stuck must focus on obliterating obstacles. One option is to try to fill the CFO void by hiring a full-time person. You have seen throughout this book the many reasons the TrueTEAM approach works better: a three-person team brings broader expertise. Foresight CFO cumulatively has many decades of experience in teamwork and management coaching rooted in our background in business, the military, and university teaching. And the cost of all this support is less than the full-time hire. Our ability to bulk purchase services and bring our own technology to tasks contributes to the clients' cost savings. Our purpose is to ensure that you generate higher revenue, more profit, and better cash flow while increasing the value of the business.

CEOs who neglect getting the help they need to tackle the obstacles are going to stay stuck. We have seen in this book how developing the FIVE Habits of Profitability among managers is fundamental to business growth. There is help available to develop these habits. Why don't more CEOs seek it out? Some first-time business owners lack the experience to recognize shortcomings in their business capacity. They may have shoddy technology or accounting systems, or have a poor sales department, and not know better. Among more experienced CEOs, some have blind spots that keep them from seeing what ails their business. They may recognize the symptoms but not the root cause. Finally, some CEOs see the work and resources involved in developing these Habits of Profitability as an expense rather than an investment.

Since we have been discussing flying, think about how most airlines fail to set themselves apart from competitors and how they provide their customers a generic commodity service. In chapter 5, we considered the need for bold moves to overcome obstacles. One example was Richard Branson's launch of Virgin Atlantic, offering an upgraded flying experience against the conventional wisdom in an industry that was competing largely on price. Having the imagination to make a bold move, develop a unique product, and outmaneuver competitors helps distinguish what we call the 2% CEOs, the elite business owners who have made it big and are willing to pay for help managing their companies' incredible growth.

Even the most successful businesses have setbacks they must account for in their financial management. Branson's Virgin Atlantic piled up so much debt in 2020 during the COVID-19 pandemic it had to file for US bankruptcy protection. During the same year, Amazon had to manage a 38 percent explosion in net sales as people stayed home and shopped online. With a $21 billion increase in net income, Amazon could easily afford to risk failure through bold moves. Remember the Fire Phone, a would-be competitor to iPhone that flamed out? The company took a $170 million charge to write off losses. A hallmark of Jeff Bezos's leadership of Amazon was giving his executives the freedom and the financial resources to fail. You don't have to be a trillion-dollar company to risk bold moves, but you do have to have the clarity and confidence instilled by having a financial flight plan.

The financial flight plan projects ahead over multiple years, so it naturally includes some aspirations that feel distant and hard to focus on. Looking at the numbers and what is achievable in the year ahead helps cut through the ambiguity. It's like flying through a fog that is gradually lifting and finally getting a clear view of a shining skyline.

Is it the promised land, where everyone loves each other? No. It's a view of your company's future in which people are working together better and are more focused on top priorities. Decision makers are asking for and receiving numbers that give them clarity. Some of the numbers inevitably will be troubling, but they will be in plain sight, well understood, and hard to deny. There can be only one response: plan to get ahead of the trouble.

Developing Trust

Throughout this book we have talked about the personal impact on CEOs of facing obstacles to business growth. Feeling stuck. Having blind spots. Lacking clarity and confidence. Some business owners we meet have fallen deep into the trap of overdependence, and our initial conversation with them may go something like this:

"How many days a week do you work?"

"I work eight days a week."

"When was the last time you went on vacation?"

Long pause. "I get away sometimes."

"But can you get off email and turn off your cellphone when you get away?"

Long pause. "If I could do that, maybe I'd still be married."

Understanding the business owner's motivation, wishes, and needs is a crucial part of developing a financial flight plan, so a Growth CFO must develop an authentic personal relationship as a trusted partner of the CEO. Of course, we also must thoroughly understand each company's financial management practices. We ask the CEO questions like, "What financial reports are you getting from your accounting managers? Are they easy to read? What do you do with those reports? Who else looks at them? What do you normally do to plan financially for a new year?" The process is systematic, takes work, and develops new Habits of Profitability. We learn what the business owner needs in terms of more disciplined financial management practices, but the conversation almost always focuses on the CEO's top-of-mind business objectives. Do they need to increase sales, find more clients, develop new products, enter new markets, or plan for succession or an acquisition?

Eliminating the CFO Void

CEOs often get overwhelmed with possible solutions to their pain points. They have hired consultants who gave them long lists of action items. Their people have come to them with initiatives they were sure would be the silver bullet, but the CEO has grown gun-shy after too many misfires. At Foresight CFO, we are not consultants or advisors. Instead, we take hands-on responsibility for filling the Growth CFO void that we described in chapter 4, and we can stay with you throughout the journey from business start-up to seeing through succession options—Getting Paid Twice. Our role is to help sort through any options dispassionately and figure out which ones are right for your company. But we don't just help with the initial evaluation. We measure how the investment in a new initiative is performing month after month, and if it's not going according to plan, the CEO has the visibility to proactively change the plan. We don't have all the answers, but we know how to look at the numbers, and we know when and how to bring in experts. We can evaluate the cost of interventions needed when actions are not bringing the expected outcomes.

A Foresight CFO TrueTEAM guides business owners across the full journey from mastering the foundations of financial management through the Seven Succession Options. As smart as CEOs are, there is no way all the analysis and decision-making required through this journey could be in one person's comfort zone. Consider how fast our world is changing—artificial intelligence, virtualization of the global workforce, automation replacing labor, blockchain, and more. We provide every team member at Foresight CFO three hours of development per week to keep up with marketplace changes, new products, and other rapid developments. We also have created proprietary technology to enable our team leads to track and follow through the plans we work side by side with CEOs to implement.

WHY BOLDNESS IS IMPORTANT

The top 20 percent of businesses generate 90 percent of the profits for that industry, which amounts to 30 times more profit in total than the other 80 percent generate.[9] Business owners who are not in that fortunate 20 percent (you know who you are!) may think they can get there someday by working hard and sticking to the fundamentals.

---

9   Chris Bradley, Martin Hirt, and Sven Smit for McKinsey & Company, *Strategy Beyond the Hockey Stick* (Hoboken, NJ: John Wiley & Sons, 2018).

Lots of research done by the big consulting firms belies that optimism. Only 8 percent of businesses will ever "graduate" into the top quintile. The ones that do so get there by making bold moves. In fact, they double their chance of advancing into the top quintile by making just one or two bold moves, and if they make three or four bold moves, they are six times more likely to make it into that top 20 percent.

Achieving Objectives

Everything we do comes back to achieving objectives. I have talked with people working in client companies who told me they were doing something new. I asked why, and they had no idea. "They just told me to do it," some will say. Maybe some consultant sold their boss a flavor-of-the-month program. "Is it working?" I ask. Again, they have no idea. Daily priorities are set by whatever comes into the email inbox rather than by long-term objectives.

The KPIs associated with our financial flight plans are clearly connected to one or a few multiyear, companywide objectives. The frontline employees are taking ownership of those objectives as they help compile the numbers that we use to track outcomes. They have a good sense of why they are doing what they are doing. It's like they are watching the scoreboard in a game where they know whether their team is ahead or behind. We also are helping management see whether employees have what they need to succeed. If the numbers are disappointing, do the employees need more training, resources, or something else? This follow-through is crucial, because without it the KPIs become meaningless. Projects drag on with no deadlines met, no milestones achieved, and no accountability.

We have shown in this book that business owners have a variety of personal motivations, but their business objectives largely match one of these five general descriptions: winning new customers, keeping and growing existing customers, having the right people and capacity to deliver effectively, achieving top financial performance, and gaining access to capital at favorable terms. A Foresight Growth CFO can provide a CEO clarity and confidence to work on any combination of these objectives. On a personal level, we want you to do what you set out to do in your business, so we would work with you on focusing on one or two top priorities at any given time. Ultimately, the goal is to give you peace of mind, more time because the business is not overly dependent on you, and financial freedom to do what you want when you want.

Feeling Grateful

Our clients have thanked us for lifting the burden of having too many priorities and no clear destination. They have been relieved from operating in a CFO void, with its blind spots and lack of good numbers that they could understand and act upon. The CEO of the Australian company that successfully expanded internationally had to overcome a lot of concerns on his team about competing in mature markets such as the US and UK. He felt that by developing good financial management habits with us, he could overcome that doubt. "Thank you. I feel like I have permission to be bold," he said.

I would be remiss if I didn't acknowledge what we get out of our work. As the best-selling author Jordan B. Peterson wrote in *12 Rules for Life*, "Do what is meaningful to you, and you will feel better about existing." We enjoy giving CEOs peace of mind, especially as you scale up your business and lose line of sight over all your operations, and financial freedom to do what you want when you want. We feel good about protecting you from being blindsided by potential downsides. Helping ensure your business isn't overly dependent on you gives you the time that we also cherish spending with family, friends, and other interests in life. We all want to feel that we are here for some greater purpose. When I can leverage my experience in the military, teaching, and building private businesses to deliver impact or "wow" a client, it's personally rewarding. But beyond that I want to establish Growth CFOs globally as my legacy.

I'm grateful to you for reading this book and look forward to talking with those of you who want more information. I hope one day a Foresight CFO TrueTEAM can work side by side with you to Obliterate Obstacles to Growth.

Experience the TrueTEAM Way

How We're Different

Working with us is a completely different experience—why just have a CFO when you can have a three-person TrueTEAM that goes well beyond any one person's comfort zone?

Our unique TrueTEAM approach will

- obliterate obstacles,

- establish the habits of financial management, and

- develop managers.

We work side by side with you to plan and follow through in 90-day sprints.

We have six goals to achieve when you work with us:

1. **Win new customers.** We'll work with your customer acquisition team to assess customer segments (80/20), optimize pricing, and align your market approach.

2. **Build capacity.** We'll develop managers to use the Habits of Profitability financial management skills, establish the current versus future org chart, assess the use of KPI dashboards, and assess the use of process/systems then implement the next steps.

3. **Proactively gain access to capital.** We'll assess the current and future need for working capital, growth, funding and reserves. Building relationships early is a bold move. It provides feedback, creates options, and expands industry contacts.

4. **Achieve positive cash flow.** We'll measure the cash conversion cycle and use the 12-week cash forecast to fuel growth ambitions safely.

5. **Engineer profitability.** We'll teach your managers to use the monthly financials like a scoreboard and run budget "what if" scenarios to figure out the best flight plan.

6. **Establish succession options to Get Paid Twice.** We'll start with the end in mind then create a strategic financial flight plan to get there. This includes developing eight drivers that make your business 71 percent more valuable and how to establish tax strategies to do well.

Change is accelerating in an increasingly complicated world. Not having a Growth CFO puts CEOs at a disadvantage. Visit us at www. foresightcfo.com to learn more about some of our primary services:

1. **Growth CFO Three-Person TrueTEAM**—recurring monthly service, no long-term agreement. We earn your business.

2. **Growth CFO Certification**—we certify both internal employees who are delivering clients services with us as well as for financial talent who want to upskill to be more competitive in the job marketplace and/or have greater impact at their current place of employment; typically, this includes directors of FP&A to CFO.

3. **Growth CFO Mastermind**—monthly learning and accountability to use current methods/skills well, plus keep up with rapid developments and capabilities. This is how we achieve continuous mastery.

Let us help you obliterate obstacles! Send me an email at kirk@ foresightcfo.com to schedule a twenty-five-minute discovery consultation with me.